# Chronicles from the Hall

CHRISTINE MACKINNON

Chronicles From The Hall
Copyright © 2018 by Christine Mackinnon

All rights reserved. No part of this publication may be reproduced, distributed, or transmitted in any form or by any means, including photocopying, recording, or other electronic or mechanical methods, without the prior written permission of the author, except in the case of brief quotations embodied in critical reviews and certain other non-commercial uses permitted by copyright law.

Tellwell Talent
www.tellwell.ca

ISBN
978-0-2288-0030-9 (Paperback)
978-0-2288-0031-6 (eBook)

*For Aislynn
Anything is possible.*

Foreword

LIFE IS ALL ABOUT RANDOMNESS. THOUGHTS, IDEAS and memories slip in and out of our heads with abandon. There is no chronological process to our memories. They often come, whether summoned or not, out of order, but with no less importance. I have decided to write this story in the same random way. I don't think it will be less effective, but perhaps more so. By the end you will have a clear picture of the characters involved. I have tried to weave both the people and the stories together with a common thread. All names have been changed to protect both the innocent and the guilty.

"You own everything that happened to you. Tell your stories. If people wanted you to write warmly about them they should have behaved better."

—Author Unknown.

One

THE FLUORESCENT HANDS ON MY MICKEY MOUSE clock read 2:15 a.m. I called it my "witching hour." If my stepfather was working the midnight shift, then I knew that he had long left the house and my mother would be fast asleep. If he was getting off at midnight, then I knew that they'd both be asleep. I'd been doing this for weeks now. Those hours after my 10:00 bedtime always passed so slowly. I turned on my bedside lamp, the one farthest from my bedroom door, and raced to cover the crack below with my folded dressing gown. If my stepfather saw the slightest glimmer of light, there would be hell to pay. Burning electricity unnecessarily was one of my lesser sins but I would be punished nonetheless. I hadn't slept much at all in the last three months and not at all for the last two weeks.

It would be the last night in that room, in that bed: the bed of my childhood. Tomorrow was the big day. I wasn't sure if the fluttering in my stomach was because of excitement or nervousness or a combination of both. I had been trying all day not to throw up and had eaten barely anything at all. My farewell dinner which I foolishly thought would be special, perhaps my favourite roast chicken, had turned out to be stew. I hated stew with a fierce passion and that night hated my mother even more for cooking it. I wanted to barf when the plate was put in front of me. My stomach held nothing but butterflies. Vomiting now would produce nothing more than their battered and bruised wings. They'd taken up residence in my body at the beginning of the summer and seemed to be multiplying daily. Luckily, and with some kind of sympathy for my plight, my mother for once did not insist that every morsel had to be eaten before I could be excused from the table.

It was a huge bone of contention between my stepfather and me. No matter what, I had to eat everything that was put in front of me. It was not uncommon for me to be forced to sit at the dinner table until 3:00 or 4:00 in the afternoon with a cold plate of congealed food in front of me. Our main meal of the day was dependent on the shifts that my stepfather was working. There was never any consideration given to my likes and dislikes. What the family ate was what I had to eat. The only break that I got was at breakfast time. I cooked my own, back in those days. Mostly I fried eggs or made Cheese Whiz on toast. Mom always stayed in bed. Nobody slept at night because of the crying baby. At lunch time when I arrived home from school I usually boiled wieners, sometimes up to five or six. Not a very healthy diet, but that's just the way it was. If my stepfather was working a day shift, it was a luxury to have the house to myself.

After being excused from the table that night before my departure, I was sent to get a bath and then straight to bed to get a good night's sleep before the next day's journey.

I sat up for the next few hours eyeing my trunk that sat on the floor at the foot of my bed. It had been there for most of the summer, its contents expanding with each passing day. It contained all of my worldly goods with the exception of my dolls and all other reminders of the childhood that I was leaving behind. I was twelve years old and off to boarding school in the morning. My Dad was dead, and my mother was remarried to a man who didn't want me around. Her sole purpose in life now was to please him. Staying out of my stepfather's way had become a full-time job for me. Since the baby had come I knew that she didn't want me around, either. I wasn't sad about it. He didn't like me and that was that. He made that clear every day of my life. I couldn't stand him either. From the first time that I met him, he scared me but pretended to like me for a little while, just long enough to get into my mother's good graces. He shouldn't have bothered. It wouldn't have made a difference to her anyway whether or not he liked me. She always said that she didn't love my father and she was determined to be happy for the first time in her life, no matter what. After a while she didn't like him very much either. She never knew how to be happy. My very existence seemed to annoy them both. Maybe he was jealous of me, a reminder of the husband that she'd had before. Keeping a low profile was becoming more and more difficult, however. He was often cruel and abusive. I was a quiet and introverted child but no matter how hard I tried nothing changed. He wouldn't or couldn't love me.

"You're more trouble than you're worth," my mother was very fond of saying.

I knew that wasn't quite true. I was never too much trouble when she was tired and didn't want to get up in the middle of the night to rock the baby or walk the floors with him for hours. He had colic and cried pretty much all day and all night. I had to take him out every afternoon for a two-hour walk in his carriage. I missed my friends that summer. They were out having fun and I was stuck with my stepfather's pride and joy. I was baffled by the fact that this screaming, red-faced little germ could be anybody's pride and joy. Besides, my stepfather never paid much attention to him anyway. When he wasn't working he was sleeping before or after a night shift, eating copious amounts of food, smoking or watching television. My Yogi Bear and Woody Woodpecker cartoons had long been replaced by the evening news and Gunsmoke and Perry Mason.

I was always busy cleaning up the dinner dishes every night and finishing up the ironing that my mother didn't get done during the day because the baby was "too fussy." It was important, he said, that I earn my keep. Mostly she was napping with my stepfather while he rested up for the next night shift or out shopping while I was doing my baby-carriage duties.

My trunk was to be picked up very early in the morning and delivered to the train station and then on to the hall, where hopefully it would be in my new room before I arrived. It was packed as it was to be unpacked: sheets, nighties and clean underwear in the top tray and lots of brand-new coordinating outfits followed by heavy winter boots and coats. No daughter of Verna's was going off to boarding school without the finest clothing and shoes that money could buy. What I wore was the most important thing of all to her as I embarked on this new chapter of my life. I had outfits to mix and match, a new one for every day for at least thirty days. She'd spent hours going over and over what had to be worn with what. Most of my shoes were colour matched, but if not, never black with brown, never grey with brown, never green with black, never beige with black and on and on. If nothing else, I should be grateful for her good, but rather obsessive, fashion sense.

The most special thing in my trunk was my set of new bed sheets. Unlike most girls at the hall, I would not be lying on the industrial whites that they provided for all new residents. I had the most beautiful sheets that ever were. Patterned sheets were not the norm back in those days. Graceful ballerinas wearing tiaras and pink and blue tutus danced on a white background. I looked at them then and couldn't wait until the next night, when I would finally lie on them and not have to worry about the baby waking up or my stepfather yelling at me, and maybe—just maybe—the butterflies would finally go away. Every bad thing that had ever happened to me in the past six years would dance out of my head and I would be as carefree as those beautiful ballerinas.

Years later I made a quilt from those well-worn sheets and it's still on my bed. Although threadbare and torn, it's a security blanket of sorts, I suppose. I'll never part with it.

I finally turned off the light and snuggled down under the old purple and gold satin eiderdown. I had fought long and hard to take it with me to the hall, but my mother said that it was too stained and old and "No meant no." I covered myself with it all winter and during the hottest nights of summer. I'm not sure why, but it reminded me of my father. Maybe he had loved it, too. I don't really remember now, but that must have been the reason that I put up such a fight to bring it with me. I lost that fight, but in the end, I won the battle. After Christmas vacation, I returned to the hall with that eiderdown. I have no idea why my mother relented, but in the end, it sat at the foot of my bed. After making it up every morning I shaped it into a butterfly before going down for breakfast.

Every last article of clothing, including my panties, had been labelled with my name: Christine Mary Hearn.

One of the girls at the hall from the Southern Shore had a father who owned the general store in the little town where they lived. These families who owned such businesses were often the most prosperous in their small communities. We all talked about her because he had given her enough panties for every day that she would be away from home, approximately one hundred pairs for each term. At the end of each day she would promptly throw the soiled ones down the garbage chute. Meanwhile, we would be busy washing out our "smalls" in one of the tiny sinks contained in each room. We often developed blisters on our fingers from scrubbing them with a bar of yellow Sunlight soap. The nuns would have been horrified by such squandering, but squealing was akin to murder among the residents of the hall and so no one ever told. I suppose we were all a little jealous of her panty wealth.

We also learned early on that first year, from older residents, that certain words could no longer be used upon entry to the hall. "Underpants" became "panties," "brassieres" became "bras," "slacks" became "pants," "stockings" became "nylons," "blouses" became "shirts" and the list went on. It was important to fit in and fitting in was everything.

Two

MY FIRST VIEW OF MCAULEY HALL WAS in September of 1966. I was there to spend my high school years within its hallowed walls along with about eighty-five other girls. The numbers fluctuated somewhat over time. Some girls were agonizingly homesick and never returned after their first long weekend at home. Some didn't even make it past the first week. Others were then added. By the middle of my senior year, the numbers had dwindled significantly. The year following my graduation, it became a residence for young female Catholic university students.

Our every move would be monitored by the Sisters of Mercy who ran the establishment. The building was as far from the mansion-like Victorian structures that we've all seen in the movies as it could possibly be. It was a relatively new three-storey red brick building built in that well known but rather ugly style that was favoured in the 1950s. It had a wide front with two smaller wings jutting out on each side and was approached by a circular drive with some grass around the perimeter. It was unadorned, with no markings to denote its purpose or religious affiliation. There were no tree-lined avenues or statuary for us. "Spartan" is the best word that I can use to describe it. A few limp tulips that bloomed every spring finished off the rather depressing facade. The two top floors at the front and back and the wing to the right housed the residents. The wing to the left was the convent where the nuns resided. It was hidden behind the large high school in the heart of the Roman Catholic precinct of St. John's, which was at the time the most valuable property in the city.

We were connected to that high school by a long, unheated overpass. The high school was probably the scariest part of my new adventure. It was the largest high school in Eastern Canada and had the capacity for 1500 students. It was called Holy Heart of Mary Regional High School. Girls from the city attended, but along with them, girls from the outlying communities were bused in. Its sheer size was intimidating. I knew of the school because my sister—who was nine years older—had attended and was a member of the first graduating class. I attended a neighbourhood elementary school. We still lived in St. John's back in those days.

The high school itself was state-of-the-art for its time. It had every modern amenity, including a large gymnasium, a theatre, an audiovisual room, elevators (for the use of nuns only), kitchens for home economics, a large sewing room with dozens of machines, a soundproof music room, a fully equipped band room, a large library, a large cafeteria, fully equipped classrooms for business students and the finest chemistry and physics labs.

The overpass meant that we would never have to wear coats or boots to school and never venture outside, no matter how bad the weather.

I can only imagine what the school must have looked like to some of the girls at the hall, the girls who came from small, isolated communities where one-room schooling was the norm. Of the eighty-five girls at the hall, there were only a handful who attended of their own accord. Most of the girls were granted bursaries to attend a high school from which they could graduate. The small communities where they grew up did not have high-school educators. The general feeling from those girls was that anybody who attended willingly and could still be at home in the bosom of their family had to be a little crazy. After all, who would leave home if they didn't have to? For that reason alone, I was a bit of an anomaly. Because of my abundant wardrobe and because I wasn't receiving a bursary, it was immediately assumed that I had come from a rich family. I had to put up with a fair amount of initial resentment, but I worked hard to fit in. Some of the girls came from communities with very few amenities, some not even having the luxury of electricity. These were the years that changed the face of Newfoundland forever, with the institution of Joseph Smallwood's resettlement program. Most came from families who lived off the fishery and the meagre harvest that the rocky shores provided.

After my father's death, I received a pension that was more than enough to pay for my room and board and anything else that I might need.

There was a strict dress code at school. Our uniform consisted of a brown jumper, with the initials HHM embroidered on a blue heart sewn just above our own. It was to signify the name of our school, Holy Heart of Mary. We wore a soft blue blouse under the jumper, white ankle socks over flesh-coloured hosiery, and brown and white saddle shoes. The jumper could fall no shorter that three inches below the knee and bare legs were not permitted. Often rulers were brought out by the nuns to measure and make sure that no one was breaking the rules. The jumper had a wide pleat at the front to disguise any developing womanly curves. I was tall for my age, so my jumper had to be handmade. It was not quite right, however, and looked—at least in my eyes—quite different from those of the other girls. The pleat in the front was in the wrong place and cut a little higher than the others. I thought that it was very unflattering. Jewellery of any kind was strictly forbidden.

The girls that were in their final year were permitted to wear a school ring. I had inherited my sister's, and when I went out after school I sometimes wore it so that I would appear older and more mature.

Although born and raised in St. John's, we moved to the airport town of Gander where my stepfather was employed. I had the advantage of being used to modern schools. But now I was coming back to my native city and leaving my family behind. I was also leaving behind an unwelcoming town, the burdens of babysitting, and the housework that I had to do. Leaving home, for me, was a small price to pay in exchange for my freedom and the pain that never left my stomach. I was never allowed to cry or show any sign of childishness or weakness at home. My stepfather was a large and fearful man. To say that I was terrified of him would be an understatement.

That first year a number of us got our ears pierced. I pierced my own with a large safety pin. I got a reputation for having more nerve than a lot of the other girls and very quickly became the resident ear piercer. Over those years I probably pierced dozens of girls' ears, and over time managed to acquire many tools of the trade. Cathy, whose father was a doctor, managed to get me a bottle of freezing spray in exchange for free piercing. I usually took food for services rendered. Food at the hall was a more valuable commodity than money. To hide the small gold rings called sleepers that couldn't be removed for six weeks after piercing, we bought pale blue headbands to cover our ears during school hours. Inevitably, some girls were caught, and forced to remove the rings and hand them over to the teachers. There were cases where the sleepers were torn from a girl's ears by nuns, leading to pain and infection. Infections were not uncommon anyway, because the newly pierced ears had to be covered all day with those headbands. A lot of the girls, including myself, had swollen glands down the sides of our necks because our poor little ears were not allowed to "breathe." Back at the hall for those first six weeks we always remembered to wear our hair down so the sleepers wouldn't be discovered. But this one act of rebellion was remarkably gratifying, despite the pain.

Unfortunately, pantyhose did not come to our part of the world until the late sixties, so until then we were forced to wear girdles with suspenders to keep up our nylons. The wearing of girdles rather than a simple suspender belt was encouraged because it limited the jiggling that could occur when we walked. Once a year, the brown jumper was dry cleaned. Our blouses were scrubbed weekly. They were made from that wonder fibre of the sixties called Banlon, which, luckily, needed no ironing. The fabric did not repel sweat, however, and the resulting stink amidst many hundreds of pubescent girls was often pretty obnoxious.

The standard of dress at the hall was just as strict. Uniforms had to be removed immediately upon returning from school. Pants were strictly forbidden. If we ventured out on a cold winter day after school for a walk, we had to wear pants under our skirts or dresses. No miniskirts (which had just hit the fashion world) were allowed at any time. Whenever we left our room after changing for bed we were required to wear a dressing gown over our pyjamas or nighties.

I have no memory of who greeted me on arrival day or who took me to my room. From the moment I entered McAuley Hall, no one from the outside world was ever allowed into our bedrooms, not even mothers or sisters. We were allowed to sit with female family members in one of the two common rooms on the main level, but brothers, fathers, uncles or other male callers were forced to sit in the vestibule by the front door under the watchful eye of the nun who operated the switchboard.

I do remember that I would not hug my mother goodbye. She did not deserve such a show of affection, as far as I was concerned. I have no idea if she was hurt by my rebuff or not. Although I was anxious to leave home, I knew in my heart that she was deserting me. I could feel her relief when she dropped me off. It was a physical thing. She knew it and I knew it. I suspect that constantly running interference between me and my stepfather was beginning to wear on her. I do remember, however, feeling free, mature, and independent. It was a glorious moment. I would not see Mom again for four months.

Three

BEFORE GOING ANY FURTHER, I FEEL THAT it's important for you to understand the absolute power of the Roman Catholic Church in Newfoundland.

In recent years, through books, movies and television, the world at large has become more and more aware of this fact. Through revelations of abuse and cover-ups, people now have a better understanding of the almost cult-like nature of the church before and during those times, and the unbelievable stature and worship given to those in its hierarchy. The subsequent code of silence went through all aspects of government and law enforcement in St. John's. Things have begun to change. Cities like Boston and Baltimore and the whole country of Ireland were victimized more than most because of their predominately Roman Catholic population.

So many lives have been altered forever by the abuse inflicted upon boys and girls alike by these so-called men and women of God.

Magnify this ten-fold when you think of Newfoundland. The very nature of an island makes an insular society even more vulnerable to the abuse of absolute power. We revered priests, nuns and Christian Brothers alike. To be an altar boy was the ultimate aspiration of every young Catholic boy. Girls were farther down the list because of the very nature of their femininity and held no place of honour unless a girl chose the convent life as her future vocation. To be singled out for any reason, to be given special attention by any of these people, was the highest honour that could be bestowed upon us.

The Roman Catholic Church was the richest land owner in the province and the most valuable of all their lands took up several square miles in the heart of the city of St. John's. It was then known as the Catholic Precinct and was presided over by the archbishop of the time. The pulse of the precinct was the Basilica of Saint John the Baptist. McAuley Hall was but a ten-minute walk away. We were surrounded by Holy Heart of Mary Regional High School for Girls, Belvedere Orphanage, Saint Patrick's High School for Boys, Gonzaga High School for Boys, two monasteries for Christian Brothers, the Mother House of the Sisters of Presentation, another convent for the teaching sisters of the Presentation Order, and Saint Michael's Convent which housed the Sisters of Mercy who looked after the orphans at Belvedere. Attached to the basilica on one side was a building known as "The Palace," which was the primary residence for the Archbishop of the diocese. On the other side was a glebe house for priests. A little farther away, below the basilica, was the Mercy Convent School for Girls, formerly a high school, but by my time it had become a middle school. This school also had an attached convent. In the other direction and taking up many acres was Belvedere Cemetery where my father is interred. There were also clubhouses used by different Catholic men's organizations.

There was a magnificent tree-lined avenue leading up to Belvedere Orphanage. Some of the older convents had beautiful formal gardens within their stone walls. I took a walk through the old precinct quite recently. Most of the land has now been sold off to wealthy investors who have built costly townhouses and apartments. Some of the land—once adorned with lovely statuary and horticultural specimens—now lays bare and blighted. One large block has been given over to community gardens for urban dwellers to have their own patch of the country in the city.

The church has been forced to sell off their valuable lands to pay for legal fees and settlements to the victims of sexual abuse that was rampant throughout their years of absolute power and corruption.

Four

I DON'T REMEMBER HOW MANY NUNS RESIDED with us at the hall, but there were quite a few, perhaps fifty or more during the early years. We had a Mother Superior who seemed to be semi-retired, a nurse, one sister who oversaw the work in the kitchen, a bursar and one sister with a bedroom on each of the two floors. She was also a teaching sister. Her primary job, however, was to monitor our activities: oversee our chores (or "charges," as they were called) and make sure that we were up on time, in bed on time, and that we maintained the measure of decorum that was expected of us at all times. For each of my three years there was always a different sister in charge of each floor, never the same for more than one school year. Some did not last an entire year. Perhaps the job of corralling a large group of hormonal teenage girls was too much for them to take.

Each girl was assigned a charge for each year. My first year's charge was to look after the mop room, a small janitorial-type closet next to the garbage chute. It was a hateful job. I had to ensure that the mops were rung out, the dirty buckets emptied, and the large industrial sink was kept clean at all times. The room was used by all the girls to do their own charges. It was a pretty rare occurrence to have things put back as they should have been. We were expected to keep our rooms, closets and sinks clean at all times. Saturday morning was cleaning and laundry day. Regular inspections to see that our charges were done and that our rooms were clean could be expected at any time. During my second and third years, my charge was a little easier. I looked after the overpass, and saw that the floors were mopped and the windows cleaned. This task got neglected more often than not. I seemed to always forget. It was not unusual for one nun or another to hunt me down and lecture me on the large and growing number of dust bunnies.

Laundry facilities were at the far end of the basement of the hall. Most of our larger items were washed in large industrial machines run by the laundry mistress. Blouses and all our undies were our responsibility. We spent those Saturday mornings scrubbing them on a washboard, often using blueing to keep them from turning grey. A cake of Sunlight soap was a requirement on every girl's list. During the week we would sometimes have to wash out our panties in the sink in our room, especially if we'd been lazy on the previous Saturday. This practice was discouraged by the nuns, however, who thought it unseemly to have our drying underwear displayed for all to see. There were drying lines in the laundry room, but no one was brave enough to adventure down there after dark.

The halls were L-shaped, with the charge nun's tiny room near the centre and a desk where one nun or another sat during study time. We never approached the sister in charge—or any other nun, for that matter—with a problem or for any kind of advice. I'm sure that they thought they had complete control but, in truth, they knew very little about what we talked about or any personal issues that we might have had. They were figureheads only, there to keep us in line, and all issues, whether they be big or small, were dealt with privately or discussed with our roommates or friends. Some of us tried to make friends with the nuns, but these efforts always ended in failure. I'll tell you about some of my experiences in a later chapter.

There was no nurturing, no affection ever shown, no physical touching of any kind, no measure of comfort ever bestowed upon us by these women of God. We looked upon them with absolute awe and reverence, and always stood in their presence—in particular when Mother Superior passed through the hallway. When she passed we bowed our heads and stood in an erect fashion, never making eye contact, and only looking up to watch after she'd passed. She always walked with a small entourage of other nuns just a few steps behind. They also treated her with the same attitude of awe and, I suspect, fear that we did. Their commands rang out powerfully, through a mouth that rarely, if ever, smiled.

Our posture, cleanliness, deportment, grooming and overall attitude was strictly monitored at all times. There were some girls who had less-than-perfect hygiene habits, but we found ways of dealing with this. Subtle hints would be given, and sometimes more extreme measures were taken. Deodorants and soaps would be left around for encouragement, but sometimes more drastic steps would be taken. Girls would ask to be moved to another room if the situation became too impossible.

Our actions and habits were, they felt, a direct reflection on the nuns themselves, and there would be hell to pay if anyone dared to step out of line. Modesty was perhaps one of the most important virtues that a young girl at the hall could possess. We learned from our very first night how to dress and undress without showing any forbidden flesh. We put on our bras backwards and then turned them around, so no belly would be shown. We threw a dressing gown over our shoulders to protect our bodies from prying eyes while putting on our nighties. It was a fine art, let me tell you, but I've never forgotten those skills.

Some of the virtues and methods of conduct that we practised are no longer important in this new world of ours, but from our kindergarten year onwards, the lessons learned from our Baltimore catechism were ones that every young Catholic was expected to display. With the nuns, the sin of pride was most frowned upon. We learned quickly that each and every girl was no better than another. Individuality was quashed. If we excelled at any task or talent no praise was ever given. It was instead to be seen as a gift from God, to be used wisely and cultivated for the greater good. A gifted singer could only sing hymns of praise, and a piano player encouraged to play only songs that would please the Lord.

This is not to say that there weren't teacher's pets. Favouritism is the universal way. Some nuns definitely had their "special girls," but some were picked on unmercifully. Prettiness, nice clothes or lovely hair often made a girl the victim of such pettiness and ridicule just in case she got "too big for her britches."

The nuns also had their own class system. There were a few who, for various reasons, were not as well educated as others and could not teach at the high school level. They were relegated to kitchen duties or general housekeeping. It didn't take us long to figure out that they didn't always practise what they preached. They were capable of bullying each other just as they were capable of bullying us.

Five

THE DINING HALL WAS LOCATED IN THE basement. There were many tables that sat four girls each, and several long banquet-style tables as well. One corner of the back wall to the right of the entrance was covered with a wooden structure with many cubby-holes designed to house our private stashes of jam, peanut butter or relish. No condiments of this sort were available to us, but we were allowed to bring them from home. Ketchup and mustard were only supplied in the event of that rarest of treats: hotdogs. Food items of any kind were strictly forbidden in our rooms. Gum chewing was not tolerated in the hall or at school.

Breakfast began at 7 a.m., dinner at 12 noon and supper at 5 p.m. We were served cafeteria-style at the front of the dining hall, farthest from the entrance. We could not ask for a second serving—gluttony being considered another of the seven deadly sins—but we could state what we did or did not want. The kitchen girls, when not being watched closely by the nun in charge, could often be talked into an extra potato or an extra wiener, if we were lucky.

If cabbage, for example, was being served, we could decline. No one stood by to see that we ate all our veggies, which were in short supply anyway, and cooked beyond recognition. Carrots became pale yellow, turnips a greyish white, but there were always lots of whole boiled, grey potatoes. On the off chance that potatoes ran low, they resorted to the instant kind, which resembled a watery porridge. Whether or not cabbage was being served, the dining hall always smelled of it. This odour, along with some particular others found only in institutions, it seems, clung to our clothes and was something that I never got used to. It's a peculiar, unpleasant odour that's difficult to describe, but never forgotten.

As we moved from right to left with our tray and meal we were presented with dessert. The choices, with very little exception, were the same. We were offered watery yellow or green Jell-O that always had a hard rubbery "skin," tapioca (which I still loathe) and sometimes, on weekends, a floury-tasting white cake with an even more floury-tasting thin layer of icing.

I suppose that our first night's offering was meant to be a baptism by fire. We were all unsure of how things worked and so were handed a plate with two large boiled potatoes (without the benefit of butter or margarine) and two black balls. I was very close to tears. I'd eaten none of that hateful stew at home the night before and had been too nervous to eat lunch, so I was good and hungry. I was happy enough to be away from the dreaded family dinners that I had been forced to endure at home and was really looking forward to some good food and meeting some new friends. I knew from my mother's kitchen that we had been given some sort of blood pudding. They were cooked till they resembled charred lumps of coal. I was a picky eater to begin with, one more thing that drove my stepfather crazy. Just a few months before, I had been forced to sit at our dinner table at home and eat corned beef hash. I hated corned beef hash. On that particular night I wasn't feeling too well but I was too afraid to tell my mother about it. I ended up vomiting the contents of my stomach all over the dinner table. The ensuing cursing and yelling from my stepfather will never be forgotten. I do remember lying in bed later that evening and smiling to myself at the look on his face after I'd spewed all over his plate of food. It made being sick worthwhile.

Back to the black balls. After every meal we were required to bring our plates up to the dishwashing area to dispose of our scraps in the slop bucket. It was a huge green bin that sat on the counter and contained leftovers and any liquids that hadn't been consumed. There hadn't been much eaten that night by any of the girls. I don't think that I need to tell you what the contents of that bucket looked like on that particular evening. The black balls floated around in the mixture of grey tea and green Jell-O.

After that we had to stack our dirty dishes that were then loaded into a large industrial dishwasher by the kitchen staff. The kitchen girls were the only laypeople who worked at the hall. These were the only smiling faces that we encountered unless the nun in charge was hovering. They dared not smile in her presence. They were intimidated by her as much as we were.

During those years at the hall we were never served fresh milk. A watery, grey, powdered milk was available, but I could never bring myself to drink the loathsome concoction. Most girls hated it. The rumour was that it was laced with saltpeter. Saltpeter, I later learned, is one of the ingredients used in making gunpowder. Back then it was often used in institutions that housed a largely male population to deter homosexual activity. Apparently prisons, boys' schools and the military used it liberally to suppress sexual urges. I suppose the nuns thought that it would do no harm and possibly work to keep us pure and prevent any sexual shenanigans. The drink of choice for most of us was tea whitened with canned milk.

I suspect that most of the girls in attendance that night have never forgotten that first meal. The food, unfortunately, did not improve with time. We were never offered fresh fruit of any kind and the only source of Vitamin C that comes to mind was apple juice made with a powder that we were served in the mornings. The apple flavour definitely did not shine through. Breakfast consisted of gluey, lumpy porridge, sometimes very grey hard-boiled eggs and toast that had been made in advance and kept in the giant steamers. It was served soggy and barely toasted. Are you seeing a pattern here? Grey was our new food group. The smart girls lingered before coming down to breakfast in hopes that the staff would run out. They would then pop some bread into the toaster. It didn't happen often, but when it did it was a rare and wonderful treat. We had baker's bread that came in long plastic bags available at every meal, and often times it was the only thing that I found edible. Within weeks we heard that the girls at Belvedere Orphanage got homemade bread every day. We were very jealous indeed.

The largest meal of the day was served at noon and the meals never varied much from week to week. Watery stew, pea soup, corned beef and cabbage, fried bologna, baked beans and the obligatory two meals of fish per week were the norm. That first term I think I packed on about twenty pounds because I existed primarily on bread and potatoes. Once in a while the cooks got adventurous and made stuffed bologna and fish cakes instead of the usual dried cod fish. When I returned home for that first Christmas, my mother asked me if I had any good recipes to pass along. She saw that I'd put on some weight and, I suppose, thought that I was dining on gourmet meals. I never complained to her, though. It was still better than being at home.

Six

As I mentioned earlier, a lot of my hall-mates were there because they wanted to attend high school, and this was the only option open to them. Some of the communities that they came from were only accessible by coastal boats. The resettlement program hoped to give the residents of these small, remote outports a better quality of life with readily available healthcare, better education, sewers, water, power and other amenities that had not been previously available to them. It was life-changing for so many Newfoundlanders. Its merits, however, are still being debated.

Obviously, the girls from these communities had lived a much simpler life than I had. It was a mistake, however, to think that their hand-me-down clothes and thick Irish-like brogues made them less intelligent or backward-thinking.

Back in the sixties, the term "dumb Newfie" was coined. The city of Toronto was inundated with Newfoundlanders ready and willing to work. Because they spoke differently and always had smiles on their faces they were somehow perceived to be slow or backward. It was an unfair observation, to be sure, but a real one nonetheless. Nothing could have been further from the truth. The Roman Catholic children of my generation benefited from a superior education from the Sisters of Mercy, the Sisters of Presentation and the Christian Brothers, and we have to be grateful for that, despite the scandals and abuses that were uncovered in later years,.

At least a dozen of the girls were from Merasheen Island, which is located off the Southern Shore. It is remote, but a very beautiful place, I'm told. It took a lengthy taxi drive and then another long journey by coastal boat to reach the island. Nobody missed home more than those girls. I longed to go with them for a long weekend, knowing that I'd be welcomed, but I could not imagine such a long, gruelling journey. To them, a long weekend which offered only about eighteen hours with their families was more than worthwhile. Twelve hours each way and only eighteen hours at home made for an arduous trip. Most of them had brothers and sisters who were also living in the city and boarding at St. Bon's down the road, or older siblings who stayed in boarding houses downtown.

We heard many stories about a particular landlady called Minnie, who charged too much money and required her borders to sleep in dungeon-like conditions with ridiculous rules and invasions of privacy. I saw her once when I went to visit with my friend, whose brother lived there. In the middle of winter, we were made to stand out on the street and talk. Guests were not allowed inside. We all hated Minnie almost as much as we hated some of the nuns. Her boarding house was no more than a hovel but has now become one of the many restored old homes that make up Jellybean Row, one of the most charming parts of the city.

Edward was a brother to one of our girls from the island and was a resident at St. Bon's. We had no evening privileges during our junior year. We could go out after school from 3 p.m. until 4:30 p.m. and from 2 p.m. until 4 p.m. on Saturday and Sunday afternoons. Edward was a very handsome and older boy. He was in grade 11 and off to college in a year. I developed a crush on him even though we'd never spoken. I decided that the key to Edward's heart was through his sister who had her room just across the hall from me. I pried all the information that I could from her and from any of the other girls who knew him. I wanted to know everything that there was to know about him. Most of all, I needed him to know that I existed. More planning could not have gone into the Paris Peace Talks. Getting-to-know-you telephone calls were out of the question. We had one pay phone for our collective use in the hall just outside the common rooms that could be used for one hour every afternoon and evening. It was always in use by the older girls who had steady boyfriends. Even calling home had to be done through the pay phone. The switch board was there for the use of the nuns only. There was a regular rotary dial phone on each of the two floors, but it was only ever used in the event of an extreme emergency and never for outgoing calls. It did ring for me one night while I was writing the final exams of my senior year. My grandfather, whom I barely knew, had passed away and I was given details of the funeral by my mother and—most importantly—my wardrobe for the service.

Eventually Edward was informed of my interest and decided that we would go to a Sunday afternoon matinee. I have no doubt at all that if I still lived at home, this so-called date would not be happening. With no guidance and very little good judgement, we made some very poor choices, choices that no normal twelve-year-old should ever have to make. It was made clear to me from the beginning that Edward was a very special boy. Why? Well, Edward had a calling. He had been called by God to join the priesthood. This made him even more enticing to me and the whole adventure took on an even greater sense of romance and allure. I suppose the notions of a fairly mature twelve-year-old girl can only be understood by a fairly mature twelve-year-old girl. I was not unlike a young woman of today who thinks that she could turn her gay friend straight. Of course, I had no idea what being gay or homosexual meant in those days. I did like to pretend that I was a mature woman of the world. I was physically more mature and taller than most my age, had skipped a year in school and people—especially boys—thought that I was much older than I actually was. I had grown up much too soon in many ways, but was still obviously a child, although I tried very hard to hide that fact.

Sunday afternoon couldn't come fast enough for me. I spent a lot of my free time walking back and forth in front of St. Bon's hoping to get a glimpse of him when he headed out for a walk. Because of my stalking, he knew soon enough who I was and seemed friendly and kind of flirty when our eyes met. We never did speak to each other, though, before that big date.

A great deal of thought and discussion went in to my wardrobe choice and hair style. Should I wear it up or down, use a clip or a headband, curly or straight? Although my hair is naturally curly, straightening it could be achieved, but the task wouldn't be easy. A guard had to be posted outside the laundry room door in the basement. I needed to acquire some brown paper grocery bags to hopefully protect it from being scorched during the ironing process. Last, but not least, a volunteer to iron my hair had to be found. Some of the girls achieved an enviable smoothness by setting their hair with empty frozen orange juice cans. Unfortunately, I hadn't collected enough to set my long hair in that way. After learning this new technique, I quickly dispatched a letter home to my mother so that she could start collecting them for me.

There were other burning questions. Should I eat something if Edward offered to buy some treats? It was decided by popular vote that, because of his lack of spending money, I would politely decline if asked. He was saving his money for university. I had a lot of cheerleaders in my corner living vicariously through me. After just two months at the hall I was going on a real date with a boy, and a very handsome one at that. Of course, there would be lots of chaperones on our walk to the theatre. Some of the girls would be walking at a discreet distance behind to see how things would progress. None of them could actually afford to go into the theatre. I wouldn't have been able to, either, had I not been on a big date. I knew that they would be there and was reassured by their presence.

I was walking on air and hardly slept because of the excitement of it all. A few days into this whole adventure I began to notice some trepidation by some of the girls from his hometown. Foolishly, I put it down to jealously. One girl in particular, who was in grade 10 and known to be very sensible and devout, came to me in private and urged me to rethink my romantic plans. She seemed worried and concerned about the whole idea. I was puzzled by her reaction, but I promptly dismissed her concerns. What could she possibly know that very worldly and mature me did not?

Even more discussions took place about physical contact. I fully expected him to ask me if he could hold my hand. He may even expect a kiss on the cheek at the end of the date.

I certainly wasn't ready for that. Many different opinions and consultations with older girls took place.

At the back of the high school and just before the turn up the incline to the hall was a fire escape door that led out from the school theatre. It was a shadowy spot, even during daylight hours, and all of us girls at one time or another would spy on the older girls who had steady boyfriends. This was the location of choice for necking at the end of their dates. We younger girls were scandalized by such behaviour but were not above watching what actually went on. My room for a time was in direct line of sight of what went on below. It had become a gathering place for spying where we loftily judged those girls who indulged in such behaviour.

We had established through much discussion (as had most boys and girls of our generation) the different levels of sexual activity. First came a peck on the cheek, followed by a kiss on the lips. From there it went to the full open-mouth kiss which was saved for only the most serious of boyfriends. There was much laughter and revulsion at the thoughts of the highly promiscuous French kiss. Next came the various levels of petting. These steps were only discussed in whispers and only with one's closest friends. It started with light petting that would only occur through many layers of clothing. Naked petting was unheard of in our young Catholic school girls' minds. Going all the way was not even spoken about. No doubt if I'd stayed at home all this sex education would have come to me sometime in the future. But throw a bunch of like-minded girls together in a school where we slept, ate, showered and shared toilets and, well, boys and nuns were pretty much all that we talked about.

Until the summer of my twelfth year, just before heading off to the hall, I thought that a girl could get pregnant just by falling asleep on a boy's shoulder. This information had been passed on to me after an end-of-school outing in grade eight. I had fallen asleep on the bus ride home on the shoulder of one Joey Kennedy after a trip to the lake. I was terrified for weeks waiting for my next period. After that, my knowledge was upgraded. I was told that it happened by direct contact with belly buttons. We all learned a lot about sex during that first year at the hall.

It was arranged through a third party that Edward would meet me at the end of the drive, which was out of sight of the hall. The nuns strictly forbade juniors to have any association with the opposite sex. He stood there in a glorious camel-hair top coat, brush cut and even a little bit of five o'clock shadow, and it was only two o'clock in the afternoon. All the boys who I knew back home didn't even shave yet. These details in a boy never went unnoticed by girls our age. We talked endlessly about puberty, developing breasts or lack thereof, our periods or lack thereof, and any other information that we could gather from each other. Some girls had a lot more knowledge than others and any of the older girls who we could get close to were always eager to advise and educate. It was natural curiosity and long before the days of sex education in the school system, so we were hungry for all the knowledge that we could get. It was often inaccurate, but of course we didn't know that at the time.

So off we went to the Capital Theatre. Halfway there Edward grabbed my hand and plunged it into his pocket while mumbling something about keeping me warm. I don't remember much conversation. Before we even reached the theatre, I realized that I didn't like him very much at all. He was very conceited. That was a word that we often used in our circle to describe a boy who was too full of himself. I remember that he didn't ask me anything about myself and cut me off whenever I tried to speak. I wasn't very confident, so it didn't take much to silence me. I do remember thinking that I'd wasted three squirts of the Tabu perfume that I'd pilfered from my sister before leaving home. It was getting its premiere run on this big date. Before long I was wishing that I stunk so that he'd stay away from me. He took me up the stairs to the balcony. If I'd been a little smarter, I would have seen this as the first warning sign of what was to follow. Everybody knew that only fast girls went to the balcony with their dates and we all suspected that French kissing took place up there.

Within moments after the lights went dim, he threw one leg across my lap, one arm around my shoulder, and proceeded to ram his tongue so far down my throat that I began to gag. Even then, I still wanted him to think that I was more experienced than I really was. I told him politely that he could not kiss me and to please take his leg off my lap. He wasn't that easily deterred, however.

In no time at all he was kissing me again, no tongue this time, but I ended it quickly. I have no memory of the movie that played that day, but the kisses still stick in my mind. Yes, there were a few more after the first. He kissed me with an open mouth, which of course was a sinful act. The kisses were very memorable because his mouth felt as if was full of crumbs. Yes, crumbs!

I kept thinking, "How can this be happening? How can somebody have a mouthful of crumbs like that if they'd not even eaten anything?"

In the days after, my roommate and I discussed this endlessly. We came to the conclusion that he must have had a mouthful of warts. It was a very weird experience. I vowed never to kiss anybody ever again. After the movie he didn't even walk me home but left me in front of his school while I walked the rest of the way back to the hall alone. The girls were full of questions. They'd been waiting patiently for a full report. I shut them all down, went to my room and didn't even go down for supper.

The only person who dared to approach me was Margaret, the thoughtful girl from grade 10 who'd tried to warn me about Edward in the first place. She'd guessed, without asking, what had happened. She then told me that Edward had a terrible reputation with girls. I was more than a little shocked by this bit of information because of his calling to the priesthood. She told me that he wanted to get in as much experience with girls as possible before he entered the seminary and a life of celibacy. There were even rumours, she said, that he'd gone all the way with some girls. In some warped way it made sense to me, and with so little experience I probably would have gone on the date with him anyway. At that time—and for many years after—I often developed quick, heartbreaking and often desperate crushes on unsuitable guys. I learned my first lesson the hard way. I never did confide to Margaret about the strange kisses from Edward. Perhaps he'd picked up some kind of disease from those more experienced girls that he sought out. The mystery still remains, however, as to whether or not Edward ever joined the priesthood, but I suspect that if he did, then his calling did not last too long.

Seven

MY FIRST TERM AT THE HALL WAS probably my happiest time spent there and the happiest that I'd been since my father had died six years earlier. I was miserable, lonely and in a constant state of fear and anxiety at home after my mother's remarriage and was given little or no attention except for the many times when I displeased my stepfather. To be with a group of girls who were also cast adrift and who enjoyed laughter and fun was a wonderful gift. Don't get the idea that our life was full of boisterous good times. We were required to maintain a manner of quiet decorum at all times. This fact alone created an ever-greater bond. We revelled in "getting one over" on the nuns by having as much fun as possible while still maintaining the illusion of quiet piety. Several of us spent many hours sitting on each other's beds, telling stories, talking about boys, talking about the nuns—some shedding tears over their homesickness—and anything else that occupied the minds of young teenage girls. It was a camaraderie that probably doesn't exist in any other environment. We became each other's family. The girls who suffered from homesickness did one of two things: they kept to themselves, doors closed as often as allowed, or they joined a group to find a new family. I was sometimes unhappy, but I was never homesick, not from the first day that I entered until the day that I graduated.

We each had one roommate only. We all agreed that this was a pretty good set up, especially after we learned that the girls over at Belvedere Orphanage were still living in large dormitories. My first roommate, Helen, didn't even last a week. She never spoke and cried day and night. By that first weekend the nuns knew that she would never make it and called her parents to come and get her. By the time that I got home from school on Friday she was gone.

Our rooms consisted of two single beds with a desk at the head that filled the gap between our beds and the window. The windows were fairly large, not picture-sized, but larger than what would have been found in an older building. The old boarding school run by the nuns was out in the country on the grounds of a property called Littledale. Littledale was set in the middle of acres of gardens and small man-made ponds, with walking paths dotted with statuary. The girls, while there, lived dormitory style. The calling to do God's work back in the late fifties and early sixties was so great that the whole property had been turned over to a home for novice and postulant nuns just coming into the fold. Because of the need for housing for high school students, McAuley Hall was built.

Littledale had a beautiful indoor swimming pool that we were bused to once a month during our senior year. It wasn't a required activity. I only went once. It was an opportunity to see a few of the younger nuns in bathing suits, a sight that none of us could pass up. On my first and last trip I took a dive, feet first, into the deep end. The top of my two-piece bathing suit popped up to my neck by the force of the water and exposed my breasts to a pool full of girls and, worse yet, nuns. I burned with humiliation and never went back to the pool again.

At the foot of one of our beds was a small sink, just one per room, and a closet called a clothes press. The clothes press had two sliding doors, was about three and a half feet wide and contained shelving on one side and a place to hang dresses and blouses on the other. Underneath, there were two drawers for towels and toiletries which we were required to bring from home. Under each bed was a sliding drawer for footwear. Winter boots, skates and coats were stored in the basement in a locker room not too far from the dining hall.

We came and left through the basement door so as not to track mud or snow or rain on the shining floors of the hall. We then had to sign in or out at the switchboard near the front door. More senior girls, who had the privilege of being out in the evening, always had to come and go through the front doors. The basement doors were always locked at 5:00.

Our beds were made of green metal, the walls painted with the same institutional green—much like that of hospitals at the time—and curtains and bedspreads made of a lightweight green-striped fabric. Desks had three drawers down one side and an open shelf just above our heads. We were allowed nothing on the walls and minimal clutter. Beds had to be made the minute that we rose, and with perfect hospital corners. We could bring an extra pillow from home if we wanted. We developed codes with girls on the other side of our common wall, an unsophisticated type of Morse code that we used when we couldn't sleep. Sometimes we would sneak a glass from the dining room to try and hear words from the other room. Unfortunately, our glasses were made of plastic and we never had much luck with this technique.

As I already mentioned, no food of any kind was allowed in our rooms because of the dreaded silverfish, a crawling insect that often finds a home in institutions and is, we were told, drawn to food. At regular intervals there would be inspections for forbidden foodstuffs and dust bunnies. I was lucky. In all of my three years at the hall I never did see one of those crawling creatures. On occasion, a scream could be heard coming from one of the rooms. Invariably it was because of a silverfish sighting. We always had to be prepared for an unscheduled inspection.

At the end of the hall were two bathrooms, one on each wing. One housed the showers and a few toilets. And the other, more toilets and a small single bathtub in a little room of its own with a door that locked. That bathtub room was a highly sought-after commodity, and when possible, we would use it at any time of day or night. During the thirty minutes given over to preparations for bed, it was impossible to get a bath even if one was lucky enough to find it empty. There was a constant knocking on the door and an unending lineup accompanied by impatient calls to hurry up. But it was the only place in the hall where one could grab a few precious moments of privacy behind a locked door. Sometimes we would give up a Saturday afternoon's freedom outdoors just to have a long bubble bath.

The desk of the study monitor was always occupied between the hours of 6:30 and 9 p.m. The monitor made sure that every girl had her nose to the grindstone and she walked the halls constantly, often standing in doorways to see that we weren't goofing off. Doors had to be left open, permission had to be granted to go to the bathroom, and we were required to stay seated at our desks. Sometimes, while studying for exams, some of the kinder nuns would allow us to sit on our beds, but that was a rare occurrence.

A Millie the Model comic book or Archie and Veronica were sometimes slipped between the pages of an exercise book, but there would be severe consequences imposed if we were caught. Being grounded was the worst punishment of all. No fresh air for a week or two was more than we could bear.

I was the type of student who did the required homework assignments but not much else, preferring to cram for exams. I found two and a half hours of study time endless and boring. I often used the time to write the required letters home or to my friends. Talking between roommates was forbidden during study time as well. Very few of us ever shared the same homeroom, so we could never use the excuse that we were conferring on assignments.

There was a very small room on the second floor that contained a standard square table with four chairs that served as the library for the hall. It didn't contain much in the way of books. There were several outdated issues of Reader's Digest, some old school books (no longer used), a set of encyclopaedias and a few well-thumbed classics. If we were granted permission, it was a welcome respite from our own four walls. It was often used if a student was doing a special project. I remember one year having to do an essay on the dangers of drug usage. I plagiarized every word from an old Reader's Digest issue and received an A+. I lived in fear for months that my crime would be discovered, but it never was.

It didn't take us long to distinguish one nun's footsteps from another. They all had a unique footfall or a particular squeak in their shoe. We just as quickly figured out which one was more lenient than another, which ones, if properly engaged, would come into our rooms for a little conversation, and those who were too lazy to spend much time walking the floors. These nuns were, however, few and far between. They often switched up their duty roster to keep us on our toes. The superiors thought of us all as potential juvenile delinquents and felt that they had to stay one step ahead of us at all times.

The older nuns never took study time. They were treated with the utmost respect and reverence and never mingled with us girls. I've spoken about the beak-nosed and aloof Mother Superior. She wasn't the only one with such an attitude. There were many more to be feared rather than enjoyed. Sternness seemed to be a requirement among them. Not all adhered to this code. A few were kind, funny and almost human.

Eight

LIKE MOST RELIGIOUS ORDERS, THE SISTERS OF Mercy had a unique manner of dress. It was called a habit. The gown itself was floor length and made from many yards of black serge (unless, of course, they were nursing sisters, who dressed all in white). The habit had many pleats all around the bodice and skirt to disguise any womanly features. This was an impossible task, of course, for many of the more portly, rounded nuns. It was gathered at the waist by a leather belt called a cincture and was buckled at the side, with the end of the belt dropping to the floor. This belt had some sort of spiritual meaning and was never used as a weapon of punishment. The skirt of the habit was full and would almost—and often did—cover the feet. Most sisters wore a low-heeled, laced-up shoe in the style most often associated with grannies of days gone by.

Some of the taller sisters wore flats. Wide, flowing sleeves covered another tighter sleeve underneath. The bell-shaped outer sleeve's purpose was so that the sisters could cross their hands to hide them. Wrists were not exposed. The ring finger of the left hand was encased in a simple white-gold band to denote that they had taken their vows and were, for all intents and purposes, the bride of Christ. The outer sleeve could be removed when they were doing any labours that required freedom of movement. With hands crossed, they would walk in procession while in the public eye. In school the outer sleeves were always in place and were only flung back to raise a strap. For outdoor wear, they wore a long, black cloak. I never saw them wearing anything on their heads other that their veil and head piece, no matter what the weather.

Strapping was a commonplace occurrence in the junior high school that I had left behind in Gander. That school was run by the Sisters of Presentation who often used corporal punishment. It only happened to me once, but all students lived in mortal fear of that black, lethal-looking weapon. Some boys would be whipped until they bled every day of every school year. We had several students in our classrooms who were years older than the rest of us, kept back for one reason or another; some, I suspect, because of one type of learning disability or another. One such boy, Tommy, had had enough and one sunny spring afternoon jumped from the second story window of our classroom never to return. Tommy went on to have a distinguished career in law enforcement but was sadly killed in the line of duty. It was a shameful practice and a blight on the women who were bound to protect the children entrusted with our care. Strapping was a rare occurrence at Holy Heart, but it did happen once in a while. Our punishments usually took the form of public humiliation.

A celluloid gimp, or bib-like garment, of white covered the chest of the sisters from neck to waist. Covering the head, neck and everything but the very front of the face was a stiff, white, heavily starched, coif-like band that dropped to just above the eyebrows. No hair was visible except for those that had sprouting chins or upper lips. We spent many hours wondering if they even had hair, wore underwear or even went to the bathroom. To us, they were above such human functions. Hanging from their waist was also a long set of large rosary beads that dropped almost to the floor. The beads contained fifteen decades rather that the standard five of an ordinary set of rosary beads. The clacking of the beads was sometimes our only predictor of incoming nuns and often a sound that struck fear into our hearts. The headpiece was a black veil that flowed down the back. The primary difference between the two orders was just the shape of the headpiece. Mercy was rounded while Presentation was square.

At 9:00, perhaps one or two nights a week, one of the nuns would take it upon herself to open a small canteen. It was a closet-sized room next to the furnace room at the end of nowhere. We were able to buy a bag of chips or a small candy bar for ten cents. It was here that I came to know Sister Mary Adrian. She had a large, ungainly stature, built more like a man than a woman. Back then we did not think of nuns as women. They were just nuns, plain and simple. We wondered if they'd actually been girls, what colour hair they had or even if they had periods as did other females. All those things were the fodder for many of our conversations during our idle time. We would dissect each and every one of them in minute detail. We often felt sorry for them. Red gouges were often visible on their faces where the wimples cut into their flesh. Some looked as if they would bleed at any moment. We felt sorry for the weight of their habits on warm spring and fall days. They were definitely creatures of mystery.

I suppose that's why I became friends with Sister Adrian. It was an almost forbidden opportunity to see behind the habit and to find out if a real person existed there. One of the girls at the hall had a sister who belonged to the order but even she didn't know if the nuns went to a doctor or dentist or had stopped using the toilet the minute that they entered the convent.

For some reason, Sister Adrian took a shine to me. She was often the nun who operated the canteen. I suspect now that it was her opportunity to get access to chips and candy. She often let me help her unload boxes after all the other girls were back on their floors preparing for bed. I never got into trouble with the floor supervisor because I was helping one of the nuns. Before long I developed one of those awkward schoolgirl crushes that, I suspect, all students develop at one time or another for a teacher no matter what their sex.

I think that for a time she really enjoyed my company and God knows that I was starving for a little attention. However, before long, I became a bit of a stalker. I lurked in the halls every morning for the sound of her footsteps. Her footfalls were heavy and not easily missed. I got jealous if she talked to any other girls except me in passing. In short, I very quickly became a pest and she soon grew tired of me. She did not let me down gently. She became rude and dismissive and sometimes cruel. But, of course, I refused to take the obvious hints. I was there at every turn and bragged to the other girls that she was my friend. In the early days, I entrusted her with confidences about my life at home and my sadness over my father's death and anything else that I could think of that would endear me to her.

Report cards came out about a week before Christmas holidays began and, shockingly, I came first in my class. This was something that I had never even come close to in the past. I was overjoyed and sought out Sister Adrian as quickly as I could. She had to be the first to know. I saw her crossing the overpass from school and waited in the hall with a smile that spread from ear to ear. I told her my good news.

She acknowledged it with, "Sure, you're just the best of a bad lot now, aren't you?" as she walked on by.

I was heartbroken. Her cruelty was so unnecessary. But I should have known better. Ever since the early days of our religious education from the Baltimore catechism we were taught that the sin of pride is one of the most evil of them all. "Pride goeth before a fall." That was the end of our friendship.

Some of the nuns were lovely, kind women. They were few and far between, but they did exist. The nicest ones left the convent for a more conventional life shortly after I graduated from high school.

I did make another friend called Sister Madeline. She was just making her final vows and had come to do some practise teaching. I believe this was towards the end of my grade 10 year. She was raised in St. John's and had even invited me to her home to meet her family one Sunday afternoon. I spent time in her room at the hall, which was an unheard-of practice. There was a sort of no man's land behind closed doors between the boarding school and the convent where very sick girls or girls with communicable diseases were quarantined. I had spent about two weeks there once with a case of the mumps. A short time into our friendship she began to cool towards me. But she approached it with much more honesty than had Sister Adrian. She told me that the more superior nuns had taken note of our growing relationship, thought it a very bad idea for her to be exposed to a worldly girl (she was probably only about eight years older that I was) and that it could not continue. I suppose they thought that her mind could be changed regarding her calling to God. As if I had such power in those days. She was lonely, I was lonely, and that was the extent of it. We were both saddened by the whole thing. I didn't know her for long, but I valued those days spent with her.

When my mother found out about my accomplishments that first term she was thrilled, not because of my first place in class, but because now she could justify sending me to the hall in the first place. Better school, better grades.

During that first year I continued the habit that I had begun in junior high school. I went to Mass every morning. In Gander, it was a walk of about two miles. I went winter and summer for 7:00 morning Mass, no matter what the weather. There were many cold, stormy winter mornings when there would be just myself, the priest saying the Mass, and another girl called Ellen who lived across the street from the church. She later entered the convent.

I would then trek back home, have breakfast and then return to school which was next door to the church to begin my day. It still grieves me that the priest who said Mass on those mornings was later convicted on many charges of sexual molestation against young boys.

I suppose back then it was a solace of sorts, a way to find a little comfort, acceptance and understanding. I believed in the Roman Catholic Church and all of its teachings with every fibre of my being. I'd even convinced my mother and stepfather (who was a devout agnostic) to kneel at the couch every evening with me to say the Rosary. My mother, having been raised in a very devout family, could hardly say no. She'd gotten a bit off course back in those days, though. Sunday Mass was more of a fashion parade for her than anything.

And so, it became no hardship at all to continue the practice once I moved to the hall. Even though we had a chapel in the hall and a priest in residence, he performed Mass every morning so that nuns from both orders could attend. Off I'd go with my daily missal and a lace mantilla pinned to the to the top of my head, fasting so that I could receive the Blessed Sacrament. Very few of us girls followed this practice and our devoutness did not go unnoticed. It wasn't uncommon to find a holy card laying on my desk with words of inspiration inscribed on the back and signed by one of the nuns. I treasured these little gifts and still have some of them today. We often shared some with our fellow boarders. It was always an honour to receive one.

As I've already said, that first term was a wonderful time for me. I felt a part of a real family, had made lots of new friends and felt loved and accepted by them all. It was an alien feeling, but I was thriving. During that Christmas vacation at the end of first term, I lost a lot of sleep and again had that unwavering pain in the pit of my stomach. This time, though, the reason was different. I had some life-changing news to share with my mother. I had made the monumental decision to enter the convent upon graduation.

Nine

ON FEAST DAYS AND OTHER SPECIAL OCCASIONS, we were treated to a special meal. This usually occurred on long weekends when just a few girls were left at the hall and all the rest had gone home to be with their families. If I could avoid going home, then I did. I suppose the nuns didn't want to pay for kitchen help for just a few of us girls so we were treated to the meals that the nuns ate. We were allowed one weekend pass per month except during the month of exams. Most girls who could go home, did. When the numbers were down on those weekends, the quality of food went up. The meal was always chicken legs with real gravy, real mashed potatoes and relatively recognizable vegetables. It may not sound like much of a treat to you, but to us it was gourmet fare. Unlike the usual mutton stew served on most Sundays and canned KLIK or KAM or SPAM for suppers, and our weekly treat of canned peaches or pears, it was heavenly. On those nights we would even get ice cream. The ice cream came in a small tube, not unlike an empty toilet paper roll, but just a little smaller. There were no markings or brand names on the cardboard and it was delivered to the kitchen service door in large cardboard boxes. Strangely enough it was absolutely delicious.

Behind the cafeteria counter were a couple of corrugated steel garage-like doors. One led to the kitchen where the food was prepared and the other led to the washing-up area. The one positive thing that can be said about the cafeteria was that I no longer had to do dishes, a job that I abhorred. Even when I was sick at home I would have to drag a kitchen chair over to the sink to kneel on because I was too weak to stand. I'm sure that if I told my mother that I was ill she would have sent me to bed. My stepfather, on the other hand, was another matter. He always thought that I was feigning sickness to get out of my chores or looking for attention. The last thing that I wanted was attention. I would do anything to fly under the radar, anything at all to avoid his attentions.

The actual cloistered parts of the hall where the nuns ate, slept and socialized were off limits to all laypersons. Back then we were told that entering cloistered areas in any convent or monastery or rectory was considered to be a mortal sin and punishable by excommunication. This might not have been the truth of the matter, but that's what we were led to believe. I'll tell you more about our brief flirt with hellfire and damnation later.

The steel doors of the cafeteria dropped down to counter level, concealing from us the inner workings of the kitchen and the nun's dining room. There was nothing of interest to be seen in either the kitchen or washing-up areas. Some days, presumably because of forgetfulness on someone's part, the garage-like door to the nun's dining room was raised by perhaps a foot or so, leaving just enough space for us to sneak a peek into their private and mysterious world. The first time that we caught a glimpse into this forbidden word was shocking to all of us who got a look inside.

The furnishings, works of art, china, silverware, candelabras and other finery were in sharp contrast to our stark and humble dining facilities. My family was not poor by any means, but this extravagant and lavish show of wealth was something that I'd only seen before in movies. We all felt as if we'd been thrown into a Charles Dickens novel. There is no sound quite like the one that occurs when real silver flatware meets fine china. Crystal goblets gleamed against the dark mahogany banquet-style table. We felt as if we were looking into the dining room of a castle. The sight of all this grandeur was shocking enough, but we were simply awestruck by the sight of the wonderful foodstuffs being served to the nuns by the kitchen staff. We grabbed our food that I remember so well that day. It was pea soup and dumplings. We took the table closest to the front and gawked at the sights in the inner sanctum. Their table was laden with perhaps a dozen or more plump, roasted chickens, browned to perfection. We spotted gravy boats glistening with a rich sauce, cranberries, fresh rolls, oval serving dishes spilling over with freshly cooked vegetables and, worst of all for us, footed epiniers filled with fresh fruits of every type. The dessert table was out of sight, thank goodness. Now we knew where that wonderful smell of roasted chicken came from. We often went to the cafeteria, following our noses only to have our hopes dashed by the sight of fried bologna and boiled potatoes. I have not eaten pea soup since and can still feel that raging sense of injustice. It was easy to see now why a lot of the nuns had a weight problem. Some were positively obese.

Within moments, our spying was noted, and the door slammed down on our drooling tongues. It didn't help, of course, that roast chicken was my favourite meal. None of us quite got over the shock of that lunch-time sight. It turned a key in our minds. Our reverence and awe of the nuns dropped by several notches that day. It wasn't the last time that we got to see into their dining hold. We quickly ran upstairs to spread the word. A lot of girls could not believe that our revered sisters lived in such a way, but soon enough everybody's awe and respect dwindled. I lost my calling to join the convent soon afterwards.

Often when girls returned from a weekend at home, their mothers usually packed boxes that we fondly referred to as "care packages." My first one arrived on my birthday in February. Living in Gander, it was easy for my mother to put it on a plane and have a taxi driver deliver it to the hall for the grand total of $5. I don't remember all of the contents of that first care package, but inside was a whole roasted chicken wrapped in tinfoil, and a dozen oranges. Those two items became staples in the parcels that arrived for me over the years. Even though no food was allowed in our rooms, we didn't worry much about it. The contents never lasted long enough for us to be in danger of being caught.

The nuns never acknowledged our birthdays or had a cake for the birthdays of the month. A roommate that I had for a short time in grade 9 lived locally. She was at the hall because her mother spent a great deal of time travelling. On occasion, her sister would bake us a chocolate cake. Her cakes were heavenly, and it was no problem for the two of us to eat the whole thing in an afternoon.

We came up with inventive ways of hiding food: inside shoes, in our boots in the basement lockers, under our pillows—and we often slept with great lumps of canned goods at night. We were forced to share a lot despite our constant state of starvation or suffer the consequences of food poisoning. We all kept a can opener and spoon in our pencil cases for canned goods, so we were able to keep tins of Vienna sausages, fruit or soup to ourselves. Eating the contents of a cold can of soup was a normal occurrence. I would usually eat all my oranges over a period of just two days, resulting in mouth ulcers that made even talking difficult. It was a small price to pay for the months of deprivation.

Having fun, as everyone knows, is an important part of a young person's childhood. Fun was not on the nun's mandate. I only remember two incidences where the opportunity to have fun was offered to us. The first occasion came to us on our first Halloween at the hall. We begged and begged to be allowed to have a Halloween party. I must have been one of the ring leaders in the outcry, because I was given the task of coming up with the plans for the event. The party took place on a Friday night. We all dressed up in anything and everything and a prize was given for the best costume. There were no store-bought princesses or witches to be found in those days. We just used our imaginations. I planned the usual bobbing of apples, and, after some research at the local library, came up with a game that's now in more common practice. It involved bowls full of grapes to resemble eyeballs, bowls of spaghetti for brain matter and raw sausages to feel like intestines and other disgusting concoctions. The passing of bowls took place in a darkened room while a poem was read aloud regarding the gory contents. The Dean of Girls was helpful in getting my plans underway and she even seemed to enjoy the preparations. She seemed impressed with my ingenuity. All went well until one of the more faint of heart got a little out of control. All it takes is just one hysterical girl to create a room full of hysterical girls. Pretty soon, girls plunging their hands into a bowl full of peeled grapes became the entrance to hell, or at least one would have thought so from the screams that ensued. The party ended quickly, to the disappointment of most.

On another occasion, we were given the use of a priest's cabin out in the country for a day of fun and food. It was for graduates only. We planned lots of outdoor games and dressed up in some old clothes that we found on the premises. Even some of the nuns joined in our games and hijinks. The weather was perfect, and the day was a complete success. Several years later, though, we found out that the owner of the cabin was a pedophile, and this was the very location where he had been taking his altar boys to molest them. I tore up all the pictures but one that I'd taken that day. The memories were tarnished forever.

Mail call was just before our return to school at lunchtime. Our names would be broadcast over the PA system and then a mad exodus down to the front office would ensue. Wednesday was the only day that I cared about. That was the day that my $5 cheque from home would arrive. This was my weekly allowance. This, however, was a problem for several reasons. It was not enough money for a girl on her own in the city to keep herself in candy, enjoy a plate of french fries at the nearby Chinese restaurant or enjoy a treat at the Woolworth's lunch counter. With the limited array of food available to us this was what most of us wanted to spend our money on. The second difficulty was finding somewhere to cash my cheque. I don't know why my mother didn't just pop a $5 bill into an envelope or leave money with the bursar to be dispensed on a regular basis. I didn't have a bank account or any form of identification.

After a time, the kindly manager of a grocery store that was not too far away would cash it for me, but during those years, with only an hour and a half of free time after school, it was a real hardship to spend most of it walking to get that damn cheque cashed. Lots of times I couldn't get it cashed at all. So, all my nice clothes and shoes didn't mean a thing. I would usually have to borrow a few quarters from girls whose parents were more generous and practical. It's not as if we didn't have the money, but the decision was made, and I couldn't change my mother's mind. Even in my senior year, after begging for a raise, I was still refused. The other problem with receiving my weekly allowance was that in order to get the cheque mailed to me my mother required a return letter. "Give one, get one" was her philosophy. Sometimes she'd even forget to put the cheque in the envelope. Before long I got the reputation of being a bum. It filled me with shame and even more resentment, and I'm sure to this day I still have some unpaid debts. I used to write home in a large hand to fill up at least two pages of paper and was often chastised if the letters weren't long enough. Once in a while, in desperation, I would lie and say that I needed some new book or a special school supply to get her to send a larger cheque. The only thing she made sure of was that I had a large supply of stamps that I sometimes sold or bartered for a can of chicken and stars soup that I would eat late at night after lights out. I would also use them to pay a debt or trade for chips or Cheezies.

Cheque-cashing day was treat day. I would walk downtown and back, sometimes alone or with a friend. Water Street in those days was the heart and soul of the city. It was thriving with large department stores, restaurants, drug stores with soda fountains, and throngs of people. Today the department stores have long disappeared. Bowring Brothers was probably my favourite. When my mother came to town to pick me up for holidays at home she always took me there for lunch. I always got a chicken leg with french fries and dressing and gravy and green peas. Their dining room had a spectacular view of the harbour.

But during my days at the hall my stop of choice was Woolworths. Upon entering, one's sense of smell was immediately ignited. The beautiful scents of the Coty face powder, Yardley's Lily of the Valley and all the other lotions and potions mingled together transported me. The store at that time was the busiest Woolworths department store in North America. Its three floors were jam-packed with anything our little hearts could desire. I spent as much time downtown as possible in those days. It was a delicious taste of freedom, one that I had only gotten to explore on very special days in my earlier childhood, and never without an adult. Although Water Street—whose fate was sealed, like most downtown cores of most cities, by the inception of shopping malls—is making a bit of a comeback. For years, though, its facade looked like a set of rotting teeth in a previously white smile, with its boarded windows and shuttered doors. A few trendy restaurants and small gift shops are starting to pop back up, but it's doubtful that it will ever return to its former glory.

My favourite smell inside Woolworths was the cooking of the yeast donuts. If I could afford it, I treated myself to a gooey chocolate glaze to fortify myself for the gruelling climb up Garrison Hill to the hall. Some of the girls didn't mind the food at the hall as much as most of us. Many had lived on a steady diet of fish, both fresh and salted. It was served to me often enough at home as well, but I've never been a fish lover. We were, of course, forbidden to eat meat on Fridays. A tuna sandwich is the closest that I come to eating something that swims nowadays.

We all walked after school even if it was just to the candy store on Military Road, but my favourite destination always remained downtown. Without much time to spare, I'd order a club sandwich with a side of potato chips at the Woolworths lunch counter. It was heavenly. But that extravagance meant that a lot of my $5 would be gone. A trip downtown and a snack left little time or money to spare. It meant running uphill, one eye on my watch, with my calf muscles screaming in protest at the steep climb, to make it in time for curfew.

Back at the candy store all the girls, including myself, had a crush on the owner's son, Randall. He worked there most days after school. The candy store sold "loosies," single cigarettes from a package for seven cents apiece. Sometimes I bought one. It made me feel grownup and started me on a disgusting habit that I didn't give up until I was in my thirties.

My roommate, Gloria, was lucky enough to run into Randall at a sock hop one weekend while she was visiting her grandparents in Portugal Cove. He asked her to dance and we were all very jealous. For the rest of the year, he only had eyes for her. Had I been a little older and a little wiser, I would have seen the pattern that developed during those few months that we were roommates. When I became friends with Sister Adrian, Gloria tried to monopolize her attentions at every opportunity. When she knew how much I liked Randall, she began dating him. When another girl from Gander came to live at the hall with her sister, she made friends with her and began going to her house for weekends, and eventually they became roommates for part of final year.

From then on, the friendship that we had so quickly developed became a thing of the past. I was deliberately excluded from every activity that involved them. She told lies and exaggerations about me. It was at about that time that I found out that she had been having sex since she was about twelve years old. To be fair, she came from a very dysfunctional family, but somewhere along the way it became her mission to hurt me as much as possible. The pattern continued even after high school. Her actions pained me a great deal, and although she wasn't at the hall for all of the three years I still saw her at school, but by that time we had stopped speaking altogether. What her motives were, I'll never know, but it was very difficult to bear. When my mother and stepfather came to town on business one winter weekend she asked if I could provide a drive for one of her friends to the stadium for a hockey game. I was too scared to ask my stepfather for any favour, but that act was the final nail in my coffin. I was shunned by many of my friends after that. I never knew what she said to them, but it changed my life at the hall for the rest of my days there. It all seems so trivial now, but back then my world was small and such a betrayal was devastating.

I have no doubt that because we were on our own, and even though we were under close scrutiny by the nuns at all times, we were much more adventurous, independent and rebellious than any girls who lived at home. We felt compelled to get one over on the nuns at every opportunity. I spent most of my time with the junior girls, but after settling in and following the chaos with Gloria, I made friends with some of the senior girls. I felt special and privileged to head up to the third floor after study time and enter the world of the more mature. Carolyn was one of those girls. She was lovely, kind and very generous. I think that she took pity on me and offered me lots of treats. For some reason she came to the hall later than most that year and didn't have a roommate. Because of her senior status and wily ways, she had wonderful methods of hiding food that none of us had ever thought of. She had endless amounts of spending money and often had fresh milk to share. She used to hang it out her window during the cold winter nights to keep it from spoiling. She had worked out some kind of deal with one of the kitchen workers, so she could keep cold pop hidden in the large refrigerators. In return for her kindness I pierced her ears for her. I had quite a little ear-piercing enterprise going by then. A few nights a week I would also set her hair in tin cans. She was always as grateful to me as I was to her. I ran into her years later and it was like we'd never been apart.

During our brief friendship and room sharing, Gloria and I developed much the same taste in snack food. One of our favourites was a rare but delicious treat called "Flings." They were a Cheezie-like snack manufactured at the time by Nabisco. We loved them and tried to share a box at least once a week. There was only one store that we knew of that stocked them and we often walked several miles, rain or snow, to a store past Rawlins Cross to buy them. After my first roommate (who left before the first week was up) left me in a room alone, Gloria and I requested the privilege of becoming roommates. It was deliberated on for many days by the floor supervisor and Dean of Girls. After a time, our request was granted. We had to make all kinds of promises to the powers-that-be that we would behave in every way. It's too bad that the friendship ended on such a sour note.

Next to us was a girl named Katherine, who ended up in a room by herself after a bout with head lice. The three of us were inseparable for a while. With our first weekend pass due in October, and with much pleading and begging, Katherine's family invited Gloria and I home with her for the weekend. It was a wonderful experience. She came from a large and loving family and we had a fabulous time, got to attend a dance at the parish hall and eat some good home cooking. She had a friend that also boarded at St. Bon's. We were introduced to each other at the dance and he was one more boy that I quickly developed a crush on. Gloria, knowing that, tried her hardest to get him to notice her too, but this time it was to no avail. I kept track of him over the years and stayed interested, often running into him on the street coming or going from school, and I know that he eventually joined the RCMP. Katherine only stayed at the hall for a year and we never did meet up again.

Ten

As I've told you, the nuns lived a much more lavish lifestyle than we boarders did, at least in their dining habits. Their rooms, however, from what I've come to know, were quite austere, small and confining. They were referred to as "cells." Although they took the vows of poverty, chastity and obedience, they never seemed to want for anything. Some were busy furthering their education by taking nighttime and summer courses at Memorial University.

Gloria, in particular, was very curious to see what was on the other side of that door that kept us from entering the cloistered area of the convent. We were all a little curious but none of us were brave enough to strike out on our own to explore. Of course, such an expedition would have to take place in the dead of night. Gloria's first adventure to the other side took place one night long after midnight. She decided to go alone. With no one to share the experience with, she was anxious to have company and to prove to those of us who hadn't gone that she was actually telling the truth about where she'd been. I had no doubt about her truthfulness because of all the fresh fruit that she returned with. She began recruiting partners in crime. I was terrified, but eventually relented. The night was set, along with synchronized watches and a rendezvous point. The danger would be greater for all this time around. It's much easier to hide alone than if you're accompanied by a group of girls. Armed with flashlights that had been confiscated from Gloria's sister, we went off into the unknown. It was the boldest act that I had committed up until that point in my young life, and I knew that if we were caught we would be expelled from the hall and probably from the church itself.

Gloria, of course, having already had a few hours of experience under her belt, was leading the tour. We saw their common rooms, got a better look at their dining room, but most importantly, we got to raid their fridges. The theft was carefully done so as not to arouse suspicion. We feasted on fresh cold milk, cold roast beef and chicken, crunchy green apples and plump red grapes.

The dungeon-like darkness of the convent only fed our fears and the whole place had a ghostly feel. There were always rumours that the spirit of Mother McAuley, the founder of the order, roamed the corridors of the building at night. We didn't catch a glimpse of her that night; however, we felt as though she would pop around a corner at any turn.

In later years I found out that Mother McAuley had never even stepped foot on the island but had lived and died in her native land of Ireland. Whether ghosts can transport themselves over thousands of miles of ocean would not have mattered to us in the least. We were convinced that she was there and that was all that mattered.

Of course, seeing one of their cells was completely out of the question. The risks were high enough as they were. I was full of terror until I collapsed back onto my own bed. It's hard to believe that ten girls could be as quiet as we were that night. I never went again and don't know if any of the others, except for Gloria, ever did. At that time, I wasn't a girl who liked to flout the rules and I only went that night so that I wouldn't have to face the shame and ridicule of being called a chicken later. Gloria went back to the kitchen on a regular basis. She often brought me back a treat. Amazingly enough, she never did get caught.

Eleven

A COUPLE OF MONTHS INTO OUR STAY and during our afternoon walks to the candy store, Gloria, Katherine and I became aware that we had an admirer. There were not many residential homes in the Catholic Precinct. The land, after all, belonged to the church, but just a few doors down from the high school there were a few large homes belonging to the fire chief and police chiefs of the city. The police chief's son became a common sight on our way down Bonaventure Avenue to Military Road. We saw him nearly every day, but not in the way that you might think. He would stand in what we presumed to be his bedroom window, waving and smiling shyly in our direction. After discussions with the other girls we discovered that we three were the sole focus of his affections. Flattered is such a small word to describe how we felt. He had eyes for no one but us. We found out that he was a few years older, and that fact alone made him even more intriguing. We discussed him endlessly, made sure to make eye contact as often as possible, and before long felt emboldened enough to wave back. We soon learned that his name was Patrick. I hope that by now Patrick is happily married and bouncing grandchildren on his knee. From a distance we all decided that he was cute, but to be honest he could have looked like the Incredible Hulk. He was giving us his full attention and that was enough to make him attractive. We would have thought the same of any boy who found us interesting.

About three weeks or so into Patrick's attentions some bizarre behaviour began to emerge. One afternoon, as usual, when we looked up he was spread-eagled in the window with a limb in each corner like some sort of strange starfish clinging to a wharf. He did this for about a week or so. By then we were becoming a bit alarmed by his actions and made a pact to stop looking in his direction. All three of us were in agreement that he was some sort of weirdo and our romantic feelings began to dissolve.

No doubt he noticed our disinterest and we thought that he would just move on. The next week we started leaving the hall a little later and started walking on the other side of the street to avoid his attentions. But he was not so easily deterred. On the following Monday afternoon, he must have realized that we had an even better view of his window. He was again spread-eagled in his bedroom, but this time wearing only his underwear. This went on for a few more days until finally he decided to do his starfish routine stark naked. None of us were complete strangers to the male anatomy. All three of us had brothers whose diapers we had changed. But this sight of a fully aroused male was not something that we were used to. I'm sure that Gloria knew what she was seeing but we didn't know that at the time. It was collective shock and awe to see him in the evening shadows, back lit by his bedroom light, and touching himself in a way that was completely foreign to us. We were grounded to the spot, unable to look away. We eventually ran back to the hall and in silent promise decided to never speak of it again, not even to each other.

Despite our well-intended conspiracy of silence, we were by then having intense discussions on the matter. There was a certain amount of guilt involved as well. We were, after all, good Catholic girls brought up to believe that looking at an unclothed human body, including our own, was sinful. Why else was the hall equipped with such small mirrors? Why else did we have to develop the fine art of dressing and undressing under our nighties so that not an inch of flesh was ever shown to our roommates or anyone else in the hall? Some of the shorter girls actually had to stand on their books in order to comb their hair in the mirrors above our sinks.

After much discussion amongst ourselves we decided to speak to the Dean of Girls, Sister Mary Joseph. Sister Mary

Joseph was a fairly young and energetic woman, but tough. We got away with very little under her three-year reign. Her favourite line was: "Girls, you are uncouth, uncultured and unrefined." We heard those words over and over again throughout the years and the phrase still rings in my head.

You can imagine how difficult it was to speak of those events to a nun, but in a spirit of youthful righteousness we went to see her in her office. Our fear, we told her, was that some of the less mature girls would possibly be very traumatized by the sights that we had been exposed to and for that reason alone could not keep the secret. I do remember Sister turning her head away to stifle a laugh. We were so full of fervour and failed to see the humour in our little tale. After all, it had taken a lot of courage to approach her. Yes, it's funny now, but to us, back then, not at all.

We never saw Patrick again and believe me, we checked that window every day until Christmas. I can only imagine the scene that must have taken place when a flock of nuns landed on the steps of the police chief's house to tell the tale. Sister believed us, of that we were sure. After all, who could doubt such innocent indignation.

Twelve

EVERY SPRING DURING THE MONTH OF APRIL, St. John's Harbour became a sight to behold with the arrival of the Portuguese White Fleet. Hundreds of ships would crowd the small, well-protected harbour. It is said that back in the 1800s a person could walk from one side of the harbour to the other without ever getting their feet wet. All a person had to do was skip from one vessel to another, because they were so plentiful.

It was a beautiful sight to behold, those ships, always kept in pristine condition with their white sails and hulls, and their red and green flags blowing in the breeze. Fishing off the Grand Banks became the driving force of the Portuguese economy. The fleet was always welcomed into the port of St. John's. The officers and crew provided a welcome boost to the local businesses of the city. The commander of the fleet and commanding officers became regular guests at the homes of government officials and the hierarchy of the various churches. They spent their money everywhere: nightclubs, shops, bars and restaurants, and even churches benefited from their free-spending ways. They had, after all, just spent months at sea in often very dangerous conditions and were eager to be on dry land. They bought gifts for their families and drank and partied and added much colour to the downtown core. They were primarily Roman Catholic and, of course, away from home for long periods of time. They also had some beautiful things to sell in return, like hand-embroidered linens, lovely jewellery and the dolls of their native land.

Their fellow countrymen referred to them as "soldiers of the sea," because of the dangers that they faced everyday on the North Atlantic. They sailed away from their home shores amidst much wailing and crying, Masses and prayers from the devout, and blessings from the thousands that came to see them off. By the time that they arrived in St. John's they were hungry for food, liquor and the sights and sounds of the city. Mostly though, they were hungry for women.

We were given a talk each spring about the dangers of getting too close to the randy sailors. We had heard (though not from the nuns, of course) that there were prostitutes downtown who would have sex with them for the right price. In the early days we weren't quite sure what that meant, but by senior year our knowledge of such things had grown considerably. My mother had also warned me about them before leaving home. She referred to little creatures known locally as "toilet bowl babies," who often turned up in the bathrooms of the clubs and bars downtown about nine months after the departure of the fleet. Perhaps it was urban legend, but she lived in St. John's during wartime and said that the name grew out of that time when poor little babies were born while the Americans had a large base there. Most of the babies (if they survived) often ended up in a local orphanage. Frightened young girls with no form of birth control lived with regret for the rest of their lives. We were told never to venture downtown alone while the fleet was in town. Of course, we ignored all the warnings.

For kicks, we would separate from each other to see if we could get one of the young sailors to follow us. It took only the slightest of smiles to encourage them. They would respond in their native tongue with whistles and catcalls and lascivious smiles. It now seems like such a cruel game to play but we were eager to test our feminine power over men. Many of them were barely older than us, but they were all very handsome with exotic good looks.

Once in a while, a brave sailor would follow us up the hills and back to the hall. They all seemed to know about the girl's school and I suppose they thought that we were ripe for the picking. None of us ever had any intention of carrying the game any further and thought of it as just harmless teasing. Looking back, I can see that we were playing a very dangerous game. We always felt certain that we could stay one step ahead and outrun them if we had to. Climbing the steep hills of downtown St. John's is not for the faint of heart or body, but we were used to travelling at high speed to make it back in time for curfew. We always managed to out-manoeuvre them.

Late at night, on several occasions, they would come to the hall obviously drunk and looking for a good time. They would holler and bang on the fire escape door. Some of the girls closest to the door would cry hysterically, but to most of us it was great fun. After all, the doors could only be opened from the inside and were checked every night by the floor sister just before she retired. There were always extra nuns on duty during the time that the fleet was in town. We would also get the extra bonus of seeing the nuns in their nightwear: a long, white, flowing gown and a nightcap tied under their chin. It was much like a bonnet that one would expect to see on a woman during the early 1900s. Usually after such an episode all nighttime passes would be suspended until the fleet left the harbour. I suppose we were quite lucky that none of us were ever grabbed and attacked, but I think that the young sailors were playing a game just like we were. But who can know for sure?

Thirteen

RETURNING TO THE HALL FOR MY SECOND year was a culture shock for students and nuns alike. On October 11, 1962, hundreds of elaborately robed leaders of the Catholic Church strode into St. Peter's Basilica in Rome in a massive show of ecclesiastical pomp and ceremony. It signalled the beginning of a three-year assembly that would rock their church and the lives of the faithful forever. It was called Vatican II.

The changes in the church came on like a fast-moving hurricane. The churchgoers were from then on to become an integral part of the Mass, become more involved in the affairs of the world and take a huge step into a new era that had existed for a thousand years without any real changes taking place. We could now visit other denominations' houses of worship without the risk of excommunication, become part of the broader world and no longer be apart from or above it all. It was a complete upheaval of everything that we had been brought up to believe.

The ramifications did not hit Newfoundland until 1967. Latin was no longer an official part of the Mass, nor was it ever again taught in the Catholic school system. The priest now faced the congregation, instead of away towards the crucifix. Folk Masses became commonplace. There were many other changes but the one that affected us most at the hall was that the nuns were no longer required to dress in their full head-to-toe habits.

Returning for us meant that that we could now go out, with special permission, one evening every weekend to attend dances at the boy's high school. Our curfew was 9 p.m. We were also allowed to go to the stadium to cheer on the boy's high school hockey teams. It also brought an influx of new girls and therefore new roommates. In short, it was like starting over.

The nuns also lived under less stringent rules, were able to visit their families more often and walk in public and were seen in places that before were unheard of. They went shopping for themselves, participated in the folk Masses or could be seen playing a game of volleyball with some of the girls in gym class. For the first time, we got to see that they had ankles and hair. No more flowing robes or floor-length veils. They now wore navy instead of black, a skirt just below mid-calf, a white blouse often covered by a woollen cardigan, and a short veil just past the shoulders that was attached to their hair by a headband of sorts. We saw that some were prematurely grey, some were natural blondes and that some were actually pretty. They were human beings to us now. It was extremely disconcerting, to say the least, and I'm sure no less so for them. We could now see that they had bodies just like us and hair that wasn't shaved to their scalp. A lot of the older nuns did not take to the new ways. They'd had their heads and bodies and most of their faces covered for more than fifty years, in some cases. They were not forced to accept the new ways. During a folk Mass consisting of guitar music and upbeat hymns, one could see them visibly cringing. But the younger nuns now had an obvious spring in their step, unhampered literally and figuratively by the old ways. They were now permitted to take back their original names, the names they had given up when they took their final vows.

Throughout those years, when addressing a nun we developed a shortened version of "Sister" and called them something that sounded like "Stir." It wasn't meant to be disrespectful. I think that they took it as a more endearing and less formal way of addressing them. It felt to us all that we had become family, and I suppose that in some ways we were. One doesn't live with people on an intimate basis and not know their habits, quirks and personality traits. Heaven forbid if we addressed the older nuns in such a way. It was full name as always: Sister Mary Alice, or Sister St. Michael, or Mother Angela Marie, for example. I'm not sure how a nun got promoted from "Sister" to "Mother." Perhaps it was just a matter of age or maybe there was some other requirement involved. We just said it like it was and didn't ask questions. They referred to each other in the hall and in private conversation simply as Miriam Joseph or Maria Goretti, leaving off the "Sister." This never happened at school or in any public setting. After taking back their own names, the rules still held true. They addressed each other by their Christian names. I'm sure, though, that no matter what the circumstances, they always referred to their superiors or the sisters of another order by their full title.

For all of my years at the hall, we had a resident chaplain called Father Eastman. He was of middle age, perhaps between fifty and sixty years old, but in our youth everybody over thirty was considered to be old. He was a rather remote man, tall and distinguished-looking with a full head of snow-white hair. I don't know what he had done to deserve such a cushy job, but we were told that he had a heart problem, although he always seemed very robust and healthy to us. He had a small apartment on the first floor just off the corridor that led to the common rooms. He had a piano and played beautifully. I had a great appreciation for classical music in those days. We were often given free tickets to the rehearsals for any symphony orchestra that played in town and got bused to the concerts.

Sometimes they would perform right at the high school, but most often we would we see them at the university concert hall. Other than glimpses of him coming or going from the building, the only other times that I saw Father Eastman was when he said morning Mass at the school.

Our bursar and general office manager was called Sister Mary Coletta. Besides her general office duties she looked after Father Eastman, doing his light housework and laundry, and bringing his meals to him on trays. Sister Coletta was from the same hometown as some of the boarders at the hall. We'd been told that in her younger days, before entering the convent, she would sometimes wear an ankle bracelet. Back in 1950s Newfoundland only a "loose" girl would wear such an adornment. She had what would now be referred to as a certain sex appeal, and so developed a reputation amongst us girls. This reputation was further enhanced by the amount of time that she spent with Father Eastman. In the early days we didn't pay much attention to their comings and goings, but when we became a little more worldly the time that they spent together became fodder for gossip. The door to his apartment was always kept slightly ajar when she was inside, but we would often linger outside and never hear voices or see any signs of life in the small living room. Who knows what went on inside the tiny apartment. It always seemed out of the ordinary behaviour between a nun and a priest. No one will ever know.

Another nun, Sister Mary Elizabeth, had a good friend—
or who we presumed to be a good friend—who was a priest.
Priests of his order did not take the vow of poverty. He drove
a beautiful, long, red convertible. On Saturday or Sunday
afternoons we would watch them speeding down the long
drive to Bonaventure Avenue, Sister's veil blowing in the wind.

Another major figure in our lives was the hall nurse, Sister
Mary Elaine. She dressed in white and had a small office on
the third floor right above our tiny library. The only time
that we entered her private inner sanctum was for regular
inspections for head lice. It was a typical medical office, but
tinier and always kept locked when she wasn't inside. After
morning bell and before breakfast she came to do her rounds,
prodding stragglers from their beds to check for any ailing
or malingering girls. We all liked Sister Elaine. She was kind
when we were sick and sometimes allowed us to get away with
the occasional sick day when there was obviously nothing
wrong. We were lucky to have her on our side. She was the
only human touch that we ever received while at the hall.
She could always be counted on to lay a gentle hand on our
foreheads to check for fever, or to take our pulse. When we
were really ill she would sit and lay her hand on our arm or
take our hand or hold our heads while we threw up. She was
the one nun who was loved by all the girls.

There were lots of genuine ailments. Colds and flues could
spread like wildfire and there were always plenty of girls who

suffered terribly from period cramps and other side-effects. Some girls hadn't even started their periods when they arrived at the hall or knew anything about such bodily functions. She was always understanding and helped get them through their initial fears. During my mumps quarantine she kept me company for long hours, brought me trays of nourishing food and saw to my medical needs. Being in quarantine meant a lot of attention from the nuns. Visiting the sick was seen as one of their corporal works of mercy and, whether I wanted them to or not, any who had already been infected (and therefore immune) would drop by for visits. My only other contact with the other girls was by way of mail slipped under my door. My mother did send me a package while I was in quarantine, but I was much too sick to eat anything that it contained.

Sleeping in was something that was no longer possible, but on mornings when we had been up late whispering long into the night or just not in the mood, feigning some sort of malady was not unheard of. Usually during Sister Elaine's rounds, after being told that we didn't feel well, she'd reach into one of her deep pockets and pop a thermometer into our mouth. She'd then go off down the hall to rouse the other girls before returning to check on our temperatures. We'd quickly turn on the hot water and run the thermometer under the tap to drive up the mercury. I'm sure that temperatures in excess of 110 degrees were not unusual. She usually let us get away with it if we didn't try and trick her too often. After all, every girl needed a little downtime once in a while.

We all tried to not take advantage of her too often. We all loved her and wanted to remain on her good side. None of us wanted to imagine life at the hall without her as an ally.

Sometime during my second year I had a really miserable few days. I'll tell you more about that soon. I had a stomach ailment of some sort and probably vomited a few times. But that wasn't enough for me. I decided to go for the whole enchilada. I told her that I was throwing up several times a day and had unrelenting pain in my abdomen. After a week or so it was decided that my phantom ailment required a trip to the doctor.

So off we went to Dr. Brownrigg's office at Rawlins Cross. He examined me, did blood work and after much discussion and head rubbing he decided that I must have come down with some sort of jaundice. So yes, it is possible to pretend sickness and get out of school, fooling both doctors and nurses for almost three weeks. I never felt bad about the deception. I was too upset about other events that were occurring in my life at the time.

Fourteen

My new roommate in grade 10 was a girl from St. Mary's named Mary Ellen. Mary Ellen was one of those solid, dependable, no-nonsense types of people who didn't indulge in much fun or have time for frivolous matters. She had a boyfriend who was quite a few years older than her who was actually a high school teacher in a community close to where she lived. If she stayed at home then she would have been a pupil of his and her parents, although not really comfortable with the idea of her dating an older guy, agreed to send her away to school. No doubt they were also hoping that the romance would fizzle out. She was the oldest of perhaps ten children and her parents thought of her as a second mother to them. She talked about her boyfriend endlessly. He was in her opinion the handsomest, tallest and most mature man on the planet.

What they had was real love, so she told me, over and over and over again.

Things had changed over the summer. I had grown up a lot during the last year and a half, both physically and emotionally. I was now a full-fledged teenager, a teenager with growing confidence. I was no longer the terrified little girl who was afraid to make eye contact with my mother or stepfather. I was definitely not the same girl who had walked through the front doors of the hall at the beginning of junior year. I was now a seasoned resident, one who knew the ropes more than most. We second-years had an edge over the newcomers, and perhaps flaunted that fact a little too much. I still longed for love and attention a little too much and attached myself to people a little too quickly, but I believe that I was well-liked among my peers. We returning girls stuck together.

After a lot of begging and pleading on my part, Mary Ellen invited me home to spend a long weekend with her family. I was still avoiding going home whenever possible and always loved being around large, loving families. I was an avid student of family dynamics then, and still do love to observe and assess what goes on between them. I suppose I was living vicariously through them. Any family was better than mine.

Mary Ellen's father ran the general store where they lived. They lived in a large home, attached to an even larger shop. One of her brothers took a liking to me right away and wrote me letters for the next two years, professing his undying love.

The problem was that I didn't feel much towards him at all. He was nice, but that's as far as it went for me. In adulthood he became a successful politician in the province. I often wonder whether or not he still remembers me. My main reason for wanting to go was to meet the fabulous boyfriend. Mary Ellen talked incessantly about anything and everything. Before I even got to her hometown the cast of characters were well known to me. I knew many of the secrets and quirks of most of the townsfolk and couldn't wait to get a first-hand look at them all.

Duncan, the boyfriend, had to be seen first. I knew everything there was to know about him, right down to the way that he kissed. On our first night he picked us up in his big shiny Dodge that had lethal-looking fins that seemed to be as long as the car itself. It easily seated eight people. But he was a high school principal after all and could afford the luxury. When I look back at it now, it seems a little perverted that a working man was dating a high school girl, and with her parent's permission. I had never been on a date with a boy who owned a car, let alone one who was much older. I think that her parents were glad that I was going to be around to act as chaperone on this particular date, a date that came after a three-month separation. There were others in the car that night, but I only had eyes for Duncan. He and Mary Ellen were as snuggled up as two people could be and kissing at every opportunity. I think that her parents were very wise to put me in the car that night.

It wasn't his good looks that kept me enthralled, though. He was tall, yes, and I suppose that some would call him handsome, but that would be stretching the truth just a bit too much. I couldn't get past his drooling. To be more specific, it was more of a foaming of the mouth, the corners of which constantly formed spittle that drooled down his chin. Just watching them kiss was an exercise in self-control. It took all of my efforts to keep the vomit from rising in my throat. Poor Duncan, poor Mary Ellen. When he did come up for air to say a few words, the spittle would fly all over the windshield of the car. They did eventually get married, taught high school together and had several babies, who I'm sure drooled a lot. I'm sure that they lived happily ever after.

I did have a nice weekend, even though her father constantly yelled that my footfalls were too heavy overhead while he was eating his dinner. For months after, she constantly reminded me of his annoyance at that. He seemed to bring it up in every letter that he wrote and every conversation that they had. No one before or since has every accused me of having lead feet, but he sure seemed to think that I did. I was never invited back, nor did I ever want to return. Mary Ellen was her father's daughter: stern and totally lacking in good humour.

Fifteen

A FEW THINGS HAPPENED THAT YEAR THAT brought me to the heights of ecstasy and then back down to the depths of despair. As soon as hockey season started we began to hang out at the stadium. We went to support the Catholic boy's hockey team but spent most of our time wandering around the crowded rink and taking in the sights, the sights mostly consisting of cute boys. It was on one of these nights that our eyes met, and the rest, as they say, is history. His name was Steve, and please believe me when I say that he was probably one of the handsomest guys that I had ever met, either before or since. No foam drooling down his chin, that's for sure. He was a darkhaired Adonis but not at all conceited, quite the opposite, in fact. He came from a humble background and a broken home which was almost unheard of in those days, especially in a Catholic boy. In short, he had it all: looks, personality and a kind manner, and was a real gentleman. We chatted awhile that night and arranged to meet the following weekend at the Brother Rice dance. That was the Roman Catholic School for boys just up the road from our school. Their monthly dances always had great live music, but this would be my first time attending.

When I went to school on Monday morning and told one of my classmates about the new boy that had asked me out on a date and his name, I almost immediately shot up in the world. He was considered to be one of the nicest, handsomest boys in the city. I was finally in. I was over the moon. By lunch time, word had spread around the large school and my popularity seemed to grow by the minute. I'd never experienced anything like it before. It was a heady feeling.

My aunt and uncle who had just moved to town met him and approved. His friends liked me. I had a date for anything and everything that was going on in the social world. I was even granted special permission to go out on two nights of some weekends if there were Catholic school functions that we could attend. I finally had a real boyfriend. It was a glorious time. I was an "it" girl. We started dating in early fall and I even returned early from my Christmas vacation at home so that we could go to the New Year's Eve ball together. My mother got me a new dress made by a local seamstress for the occasion. I stayed with my aunt and uncle for that week before school began, and when we weren't talking on the phone we were together.

I had become one of those girls who stood in the lineup at the hall for the payphone every night. He would spend a full hour dialing the number over and over again waiting and waiting for someone to hang up and hoping to get the next open line. All the boyfriends were forced to do this. It was a matter of pure luck and he didn't always get through, but more often than not we got to spend a few minutes talking. While at my uncle's house we could talk freely for hours. We were only allowed ten minutes on the phone at the hall, so that just allowed time for six calls in that one hour before bed. It was, of course, best if our boyfriends called us because we wouldn't have to spend our money nor waste time putting a dime into the phone and waiting for the call to be processed. The girls would always sit on the floor of the phone booth so those waiting outside couldn't hear our conversations. Sometimes on the way upstairs to prepare for bed we could hear the phone ringing over and over again, all of us wondering whose boyfriend got through just that one minute too late.

That New Year's Eve was the best memory of my high school days. My beautiful white mini-dress (there were no nuns around to tell me that I couldn't wear one) was shot with silver threads and I wore matching block-heeled silver shoes. Steve wore a handsome black suit. We looked stunning together, at least that's how we felt. We laughed and danced all night. There was no 10:00 curfew. I was allowed to stay out until after we'd rung in the New Year. It was magical. He bought me lovely presents for both Christmas and my birthday.

It all ended one day in late spring. He went on a basketball weekend and met someone else. He told me right away. It was my first and probably my worst experience with heartbreak. I didn't eat, sleep, talk or even go to school for at least a week. I was totally unable to function. My school friend who I'd shared my elation with months before cried when I told her. My roommate, Mary Ellen, was practically gleeful over the whole thing. She hated the fact that I had a boyfriend at all. Maybe she didn't like the fact that I hadn't fallen for her brother. When Steve dumped me, she couldn't or wouldn't show any kind of sympathy. It was pretty obvious that she was enjoying my misery immensely.

Our relationship was clean and good. We kissed a lot, but that's as far as it went. It was a perfect first relationship except for the getting dumped part. It took a long time to pick myself up, dust myself off and get on with it. Unfortunately, a few other factors got in the way of my recovery.

Mary Ellen was not particularly liked by the other girls. She wasn't fun-loving, as I've said before, but she also had a superior attitude towards the rest of us. She felt that lighthearted fun was somehow beneath her; too immature for her, it seemed. Her bossy, condescending ways did not endear her to many. Earlier in the year some money had gone missing from her pocket or wallet. She reported the incident right away and the nuns handled the incident in a very serious manner. No one, of course, came forward to take the blame. As if they would. Every girl in the hall was forced to line up on the stairway and proceed one by one into Sister Elaine's nursing office. The guilty party was given the opportunity to place the money into the pocket of a sweater that was hanging there. At the end of the exercise the money was there, returned by the thief. Who knows who the actual culprit was? The girls, however, resented her afterwards. She stood on the stairway, arms folded like an old school marm, watching us all with an air of unattractive superiority on her face as we all walked by. The money didn't add up to much, just a little more than a dollar, I think. It all seemed much ado about nothing.

Shortly after my breakup with Steve, another incident much like the first occurred. It was a Sunday afternoon and I was in a deep funk. Some change went missing from the pocket of her sweater that was hanging in our room. She told anyone who would listen that she was conducting an experiment because she believed that she knew who the thief was. Lots of chaos surrounded us again. She didn't speak to me for days afterwards. By this time, I was growing pretty tired of her ridiculous behaviour towards me and all the other girls. I confronted her in public one evening. I told her that I knew that she suspected me of being the thief and that I wasn't going to put up with her bull any longer. I told her that I had never ever touched any of her money and that I had requested to be removed from her room. All this took place in one of the common rooms and afterwards everyone clapped. She became red-faced, turned on her heel and stomped out. She was removed from my room to the other end of the corridor and never returned the following year.

I believe that I was the first person to ever stand up to her, and she was definitely the first person who I'd ever stood up to. It was a good feeling after what I'd just been through. I'd been humiliated enough. But there I was, left in a room alone for the first time since coming to the hall. Girls started dropping in again, but it wasn't the same. I was in a real depression and remained that way until I went home for summer vacation. It was just after Mary Ellen's departure from my room that I got sick with my fake jaundice.

Sixteen

THE DEAN OF DISCIPLINE AT THE HIGH school was one of our Sisters of Mercy called Sister Maria Therese. She was a diminutive little creature with the face of an angel. She moved like a dynamo.

There are a lot of wealthy Catholic families in the city of St. Johns. It was not uncommon for them to have large families because of the ever-forbidden use of birth control. It was also a common practice to give a child or two back to God for all the blessings that had been bestowed upon the family. So, a priest or two or a couple of nuns could often be siblings. It was a matter of great pride for the families of the city and the province to have this occurrence. The children chosen or encouraged to follow a calling—in my opinion, at least—were often the misfits, perhaps the least attractive or perhaps the boys who may have shown homosexual tendencies. Of course, I don't want to imply that a person who is homosexual is a pedophile. Nothing could be further from the truth. But some of these men who had oddball tendencies ended up in the priesthood. I've often felt that this is the reason for so many pedophiles amongst the clergy in Newfoundland. Per capita, the numbers seem to have been unusually high. It's also a theory of mine that priests who practised this perversion made a point of going to smaller, more isolated communities to recruit like-minded young men to follow them into their order.

It was hard to find a really beautiful nun, but Sister Mary Therese fitted the bill to perfection. She had the face of an angel. She had also taught me in kindergarten. My run-in with her back then had not been an auspicious one. After some mild infraction at the sandbox one day she decided to bring her considerable wrath upon me. She brought the long blackboard pointer down upon my tiny wrists. I was an obedient child not prone to getting into trouble of any kind. When my father saw my swollen wrists, he was outraged. Nobody was ever allowed to hurt his little girl, not even my mother who was quite fond of dishing out corporal punishment when he wasn't around.

My father had been born and raised Roman Catholic. When he was quite young his father died and his mother, for several years, was unable to look after him. He spent those years in Mount Cashel Orphanage which, as most in our part of the world know, turned out to be one of the places where the most brutal assaults—physical, emotional and sexual—took place. These acts of violence were inflicted on those young boys by the Christian Brothers, supposed men of God, put in place to nurture and care for those very same boys. Lawsuits are still being settled today, all these many years later. After leaving the orphanage, my father never again attended church except on his wedding day. Whether or not he was sexually abused is a secret that died with him, but according to stories relayed to me by mother, he was definitively the victim of physical and emotional abuse. He often told her stories of being locked in a small cupboard for days on end or being left in the outdoor swimming pool overnight during the winter.

The day after my incident with the blackboard pointer, he sent my mother to the school to deal with the matter. Sister Therese approached me at my desk soon afterwards and kissed my wrists. That was the end of that as far as she was concerned, but I never forgot the incident. But there she was, not only at the hall, but with a prominent position at the school.

The first time that we met again, I laughingly reminded her of the incident that had occurred all those years before. She was polite but dismissive towards me. She held a lofty position after all, and could not be seen fraternizing with the girls. It wasn't long before her reputation became legendary. She had a temper unlike any that I'd ever witnessed before. She was feared both throughout the high school and the hall. No one dared cross her, not ever. There were plenty of troubled girls in that large school and no doubt she had a lot to deal with and a reputation of toughness to uphold. Often her cruelties went above and beyond acceptable behaviour. After any absence, for whatever reason, every girl at school had to report to her office with a note provided from her parents or a doctor. After a flu outbreak it was not uncommon to see a lineup down the corridors of the school as far as the eye could see. She would not abide truancy of any kind and to break the rules meant expulsion. No doubt for some girls that was their goal. She would threaten police action and often visited the homes of frequently truant girls. I'm sure that the situations that she sometimes found herself in must have been shocking; beaten mothers, drunken fathers and situations of extreme poverty were probably quite common. None of these things made her go lighter on the girls who came from these environments. The girls at the hall, luckily, were waved through rather quickly. She kept a watchful eye on Sister Elaine's sick list. She also had no trouble using the strap, liberally and with every bit of strength in her little body. Because of her title and use of the strap, the classrooms were kept free of corporal punishment. It was left to her by the other teachers and nuns to do the dirty work. Once in a great while we might see a student get a slap across the face, but more often than not it was just because a nun was in a bad mood.

For some reason she felt it was her duty as one of our guardians at the hall to have a talk with each and every one of us during the last term of high school before we went off into the world. She would pluck one of us at any time to follow her to some secluded and private spot to have a conversation or lecture, whichever she deemed appropriate. We dreaded these encounters. No one had much to say upon their return, but no one ever looked very happy either. My turn was one of the last ones to come along. I was working quietly at my desk one evening when she had me follow her down to the corridor that separated the two common rooms. It was dark and gloomy there, but I expect that was all part of her method. She questioned me relentlessly. It was more of an interrogation than a talk. We had all learned long ago that a yes or no answer was all that we would give to the nuns during any conversation. The less that they knew about us, the better, as far as we were concerned.

I did speak up a little, telling her about my unhappiness at home and my feelings of restlessness and about how I felt different that the other girls. And I really did feel different. I felt more mature but more adrift than ever before in my life. I had no idea what the future would hold for me. My calling to the convent had long ago left. Unfortunately, she took this to mean that I felt that I had homosexual tendencies. How she picked that up from our conversation, I'll never know. At that time, I barely knew what that meant, let alone felt such things. My lecture on the perils of feeling "different" went on long into the night. Her implications were obvious. All

I had wanted was a little understanding but was completely misunderstood. She kept a very watchful eye on me after that. I had needed guidance in the worst possible way, but she let me down terribly.

Seventeen

DURING THOSE THREE YEARS, BESIDES OUR LATE-NIGHT visits from sailors, there was a bit of excitement now and again. One night one of the girls went missing. She was very homesick and just didn't return after her afternoon walk. A distress call was sent out by her roommate and by 10 p.m. the police were called in. She was a very quiet girl and never got into any kind of trouble, so everyone was very concerned, the nuns, of course, most of all. Nothing like this had ever happened before. None of their charges had ever gone astray and I'm sure they all had the worst possible outcome in their minds.

I was the one who actually solved the case. I reported to the Dean of Girls that I had overheard her talking about the comfort that she felt whenever she visited the basilica. The basilica is a huge, foreboding cathedral and I can't imagine anyone being alone there after dark. Back in those days, churches were left open twenty-four hours a day as a haven for those in need of shelter or solace. There were usually just a few candles left lit throughout the night. Sure enough, the police found her there. She was crying, and by the time that the officers brought her back to the hall she had to be sedated. She was understandably hysterical. The cathedral after dark was, I'm sure, a much different place than during daylight hours. Strangely enough, her parents did not take her home, so she lived out the rest of her days at the hall in misery.

Senior year meant a lot more privileges and free time. There were now more girls staying at the hall who were older taking business courses, and very few juniors. The influx of girls from the remote communities was drying up, so the nuns decided to take in more business students. The high school itself had a business college, or "commercial courses," as they were called then. Some girls were even taking courses at Memorial University. These girls had almost complete freedom to come and go as they pleased, within reason, of course. Some had steady boyfriends and went home every weekend. One girl was even engaged to be married.

They seemed very mature to me. I remember one girl giving me pills so that I could stay up all night to study for final exams. I never did take them, but it does give you an idea of how much things had changed over the three years that I was there.

One of these senior girls was from my home town. She was a pet of all the nuns because of her excellence in music and voice. She was very gifted and went on to have a career in that field. Judy, however, had a bit of a rebellious streak. She began dating a university student named Samir. Samir's father was a doctor in the city and he owned a beautiful red convertible. The fact that he was of another culture did not sit well with the nuns. After some phone calls to her parents, she was forbidden to see him any longer. Of course, this did not sit well with Judy.

She went out one Saturday night on a date with Samir and didn't return. No police were called this time because her sister, who was also a resident, had told where and with whom she'd gone. The hall was abuzz, to put it mildly. The nuns were positively apoplectic. Never before had anyone disobeyed the rules so blatantly. Her parents were notified, of course, and had driven the four and a half hours to the hall to arrive by lunch time. Still no sign of Judy. Not only had she not come home but she had missed Sunday Mass as well, a Mass in which she was scheduled to perform. We hung out our windows awaiting the arrival of the prodigal daughter. None of us had any intention of missing the fireworks that were bound to ensue.

Sometime around mid-afternoon she came driving up with Samir at the wheel of his convertible. She was not even allowed to enter the door. Her bags had already been packed and stowed in the trunk of her parent's car. We were all scandalized, not ever knowing anyone who'd displayed such nerve, but most of all we'd never known anyone who'd spent the night with a boy.

At the end of each term, before Christmas and Easter vacations and before we all left for summer vacation, we were all ready to blow off a little steam. There was no outlet for us girls to have some good, clean fun. The nuns were of the mind that fun was as bad as idleness and just another way for us to get into some kind of trouble.

But on those last nights they pretty much stayed out of our way and let us get up to as much foolishness as we could without getting too out of hand. Once in a while the floor sister would chide us for making too much noise, but she usually put bedtime aside and allowed us to run from room to room having as much fun as we wanted. The tradition was that somebody would get thrown into a cold shower and held down until they were soaked. One year it was my turn. Everybody just went along with it, if only to get their turn done and over with. We picked our targets well in advance. But the victim of our prank on the last night of the last term of senior year took us a step too far.

It was the same girl who had gone missing the year before and had to be rescued by the police. We should have made a wiser choice. We didn't think that her state of mind was as fragile as it turned out to be. It was a fiasco from beginning to end.

Our Dean of Girls for our final month at the hall, Sister Mary Joseph, had gone off to summer school. Her substitute was a nun called Sister Margaret Marie. She was young, approachable and fairly lenient. We thought that we would be off the hook.

We all looked forward to the last night with anticipation, not just because we were finally getting to have some fun, even if it was under the watchful eye of the nuns, but because it was to be our last night at the hall. The night turned into a complete disaster. Our target for the shower prank was, as usual, lifted bodily from her room and dragged to the bathroom. Most of our former victims would put up a token fight to make it more fun and that would be that. She not only screamed and kicked like she was about to be murdered but became hysterical to the point of no return. The nuns came running and it was obvious we were in deep trouble.

Our trunks were packed, exams were over, and our families would be waiting to pick us up in the morning. Instead, the whole senior floor was called down to the common room where chairs were lined up to seat everybody, with several more chairs facing those. So there and then began what can only be described as some sort of trial. We were confronted by judge and jury in the form of a flock of nuns and the defendant, Cathy. I happened to be seated in the last chair of the front row.

I was asked to speak first for the defence. I suppose having been at the hall for three years I had developed some sort of seniority, at least in the eyes of the nuns. I told the tale from the beginning, using the argument that this practice had been going on for years, no one had ever been injured, and we were just having some harmless fun. We all thought that Cathy's hysteria was an obvious overreaction, ridiculous and totally unnecessary. We had even been told by her roommate, after the fact, that she knew that she was to be that night's target and was clearly aware of what was going to happen. We all felt that her dramatics were just a bid for attention and now here she was getting just what she had hoped for.

Some parents were already in the driveway waiting to pick up their daughters, and here we were faced with her smugness. It really was an uncalled-for display of what she thought of as some kind of power trip. We were by then young women, after all, graduates about to go off into the world. Each girl, in turn, was given the opportunity to speak in her own defence but I was the only one who had anything to say. Row by row they went, each girl repeating the same line as the one before her: "It's just like Christine said." So that was that. Even the ring leader, Gloria, who had returned to the hall for part of our final year, had nothing to say. I was angry and shocked. Then came the lecture that ended our final year, our graduation and our final goodbye to the hall. It left a sour taste in our mouths. It robbed me in particular of that glorious moment when I could walk out the door, head held high, and a great big hallelujah that I was one of the very few who had survived three long years in purgatory.

Eighteen

IF MCAULEY HALL WAS PURGATORY, THEN BELVEDERE Orphanage could only be described as hell. It had stood on the grounds nearby, just a short walk from us, for hundreds of years and we'd all heard tales of the horrors that went on there. Up until a few years previously no one knew much about what went on behind its old walls. Even now there are cases still unsettled in the justice system regarding abuses that took place there. The nuns taught the girls through to graduation in the orphanage itself, until the large high school was built just next door. The nuns lived in an attached convent called St. Michaels. When they began their assimilation into the regular Catholic school system, stories began to emerge about the life that was imposed upon those poor girls. They slept, as I've said, in dormitories, had primitive washing and toilet facilities and suffered corporal punishment and other degradations on a daily basis. As is the case with many institutions run by nuns, there were pets and then there were girls who were considered to be no more than trouble just waiting to happen. Once a girl was thought to be a troublemaker, it was an almost impossible feat to rise above that reputation. In turn, those particular girls were treated abominably. There was very little turnover of the nuns who cared for the girls, so things never changed much. Some of the girls were not always orphans but were perhaps troublemakers who had been left with single parents who couldn't handle them. As long as there was someone to pay their fees then the nuns accepted them. In the case of a girl who had lost one or more parents, oftentimes their home parish would absorb the cost of their board.

As is the case with most institutions of this type, there were groups of financial benefactors who made annual treks to the orphanage so that the girls could put on a show to display how their money was being spent. May Day was an important production, planned by the nuns and put on for these benefactors where the orphans were paraded with great pomp and ceremony in front of their wealthy audience. Christmas time brought presents from the community, but I'm sure that none of it made up for the fact that the girls were all alone in the world. When the girls reached the age of maturity they were often sent out to work in the community, often in service to wealthy families. Some joined the convent themselves, having no idea how to function in the outside world.

As one of our corporal works of mercy that we were required to make as part of our religious education, we were forced to visit the orphanage at Christmas time. There is a certain smell that often accompanies poverty. The orphanage had that smell and I can still bring it to mind even now. The smell of an institution is one thing, but the smell of an orphanage quite another. Perhaps it's the lingering smell of cooked cabbage, musty clothing and unwashed bodies. The girls were forced to pick their clothes from a huge room in the basement that housed hand-me-downs from generations past. They never had the feel of anything but someone else's cheap cotton underwear against their skin. That evening when we marched over, the girls were required to put on a concert for us, something that they did regularly for visiting clergy or other nuns. They performed Christmas hymns and piano pieces. Years later I likened it to seals performing at an aquarium. They had a dead look in their eyes that still horrifies me.

You may wonder why a self-absorbed teenager like myself was so haunted by those girls. There were a couple of reasons. The first was that I knew that my father had spent years in just such an institution at the other end of the city. The second and primary reason was that—from the day that my mother remarried—I lived under the threat of a life there. I was told on a regular basis, sometimes daily, that if I ever stepped out of line in any way, that a life at Belvedere Orphanage would be my fate. I never for a moment believed that it was an idle threat. After all, I had ended up at McAuley Hall, hadn't I? I always thanked God that the hall did exist, for the school year at least. Then I only had to worry about being banished there for the summer months. I didn't have to step out of line very far to know that it was a real possibility. Upon leaving school, I remained at home throughout the following fall and winter, but by spring, less than a year after leaving the hall, I was forced out once again into a boarding house less than half a mile away from my home. I had, according to my stepfather, begun running with a bad crowd. The truth was that we did like to play loud music and laugh a lot, but what teenager didn't in the late sixties? It was all good clean fun. Considering that it was the beginning of the sexual revolution we were pretty tame compared to most standards of the day. That fact was beyond the understanding of my mother and stepfather, however, so believe me when I say that I knew in my heart that the threat of banishment to Belvedere Orphanage throughout those years was a very real one. The real truth of it was that there was no place in their new life for me. The baby no longer needed constant care, so my presence had become superfluous. The nuns taught us that suffering brought about strength and those were the words that sustained me. At the hall, we were told time and time again that we were no more than bold, impudent children. At home it was worse. For many years I believed that very strength developed during those few short years was the most vital part of my character.

Nineteen

DURING THE COURSE OF MY THREE YEARS at the hall there were several groups of sisters that came and went. None, however, were quite like the Darby girls. By my final year there were four of them living at the hall. Their father was a doctor who operated a small cottage hospital about an hour's drive outside the city. The girls came from a large Catholic family with an extremely strict father. If I lived in fear of my stepfather, then they lived in absolute terror. He was a tyrant, according to the accounts received from his daughters. Of course, there was one black sheep. Her name was Maureen. The whole family had names that began with the letter M. Maureen fell in the middle of all the children and was constantly seeking attention, whether it be good or bad. She was always up to one form of mischief or another and could be a terrible pest. Her oldest sister, also a resident at the hall, constantly despaired over her sister's antics. I somehow got the reputation of being good with hair and was always in demand for setting, ironing, comb-outs or up-dos. It soon became Maureen's habit to beg me each and every night to set her hair in tin cans. I never minded doing favours for any of the girls, but Maureen was unrelenting. I had to give up a half of my free hour before bedtime to fuss with her hair. She never gave me any peace. I would hide on the third floor with friends, and even resorted to hiding in my closet, but I was her go-to girl. If I refused to do her bidding she would actually get down on her knees and beg me. Even the youngest of her sisters tried hard to keep her in line. I spent a lot of time with the Darby girls. The dynamics between them was fascinating and I longed to meet this father who struck such fear into their hearts. Even the nuns treaded carefully around those girls. No doubt they were fearful of him as well. As I've already told you, the number of girls at the hall had dwindled considerably and they couldn't afford to offend any of the paying parents.

Grooming and skincare was always a big concern for most of us. We tried to find the latest cures for acne or exercises to enhance our breast size, or to develop exercises to gain more appealing calf muscles. Early on in junior year, a group of us started doing ballet exercises. The radiator in our rooms was about bar height, and for most of those three years I never went to bed without doing ten minutes of those exercises. We had a rhyme: "We must, we must, develop our bust," while bringing our elbows together behind our backs. We slathered our faces with Noxzema or Nivea and treated our pimples with toothpaste. The most bizarre routine that we come up with was to wash our faces nightly with our own urine. Who gave us this idea remains a mystery, but we continued the practice every night for months. Somehow one of the nuns got wind of what we were doing. She just rolled her eyes and let us get on with it. I'm sure no mother would have allowed such a thing, but then our mothers weren't around, were they?

Twenty

MY LAST YEAR WAS A DIFFICULT ONE for several reasons. To begin with, I didn't want to go back to the hall at all, because of the heartbreak and hardships of the previous year. I made the difficult decision to ask my mother to stay home and finish high school in Gander. On the day before I was to leave, I begged her to let me stay. I must have had a lot of doubts to go to such lengths. It meant that I would have to stay at home with my stepfather. It also meant that I would be separated from my boyfriend whom I'd met over the summer and who was moving to St. John's to attend university. We had become inseparable. I had matured even more over the last summer, had a greater taste of freedom and spent time with my friends and new boyfriend. It had been a wonderful summer. I spent as little time as possible at home, only arriving at night in time for curfew. Going back to the hall seemed like a death sentence. My boyfriend had promised to come home at least once a month to see me. My mother didn't even consult my stepfather. The answer was no, and that was that.

The enrolment at Holy Heart had become so large that the students were informed during a giant assembly on our first day back that we would have to begin attending classes in shifts. There were three shifts that began at 8:30 a.m. and ended at 5:30 p.m. The most desirable shift was, of course, the early shift which began at 8:30 and ended at 2:30. It meant no more getting out of school when the sun was waning during the long winter months, and lots of free time before curfew. The second most popular shift was from 11:30 until 5:30, which of course meant more sleep time in the mornings and less study time in the evenings. We would be expected to do some studying in the morning but unsupervised, unlike the nighttime study period. The least desirable shift was split from 8:30 until 11:30 and from 2:30 until 5:30. It was a gruelling day for anyone, with no time to get out for some fresh air, no time to walk downtown and really not much time to do anything after study and chores and meals were completed. This shift, of course, was assigned to all the girls at the hall because we had such a short commute.

Upon news of this major change in the school system which neither parents nor students had been alerted to, all parties including parents were in a major uproar. The many students who had to be bused in had to be up as early as 4 a.m. to make the long bus ride into the city. Parents of those students doing the late shift were worried about their daughters being on the streets and walking home after dark. Of course, the split-shift girls would have four long walks each day to and from school. It was a logistical nightmare. The Catholic school board had the foresight to build two boy's high schools, one in each end of the city. We girls were not so fortunate. Parents and students alike felt like they had no recourse available to them, so they took to the streets in protest. We were threatened with expulsion if we dared to join the protesters, so we watched helplessly from our windows at the demonstrators that thronged the streets below. Thousands and thousands of people took part, but in the end, there was no alternative but to give up. The church finally intervened. Priests took to their pulpits and begged their congregations to give up the fight. There was just no other recourse. We were doomed to spend our final year trapped in a hellish schedule. Never before or since did the school have such a high rate of failure, dropouts and absenteeism. It was an unsightly blemish on the Catholic school system of St. John's. I became one of those failures, but it was not for the sole reason of the shift classes.

That year, my home room teacher was a nun who was transferred in from another community. With the new shift system, teaching resources were stretched to the limit. We saw more lay teachers than ever before. My new homeroom teacher's name was Sister Mary David. She was a large woman with an imposing presence who still wore the old habit. She was new to all of us and we didn't know quite what to expect. Her physical appearance led us to believe that she would be old fashioned and strict to a fault. Instead, we got a gifted teacher who seemed to have a real and deep understanding of the workings of the adolescent girl. She wasn't easy on us. She expected nothing less than excellence from each and every one of us. When we did excel she was quick to offer praise and encouragement, but would chastise kindly when we failed. This was a whole new world for us girls who had been dealing with exactly the opposite through our school years with the nuns. She was a joy to be around. She made sure that she was available to us all for any issue that we had, whether it pertained to schoolwork or not. Sister David was the first person who ever saw the creative spirit that was unawakened inside me and encouraged me to let loose and develop it. This was what I had so desperately tried to convey to Sister Mary Therese. She was, instead, insistent that I most probably had a tendency towards homosexuality that had to be squashed.

I believe that in everyone's life moments of change come, a shift, if you will, of one's perceptions of oneself and the world at large. Sister Mary David was the precipitating factor for just such a shift in me. She saw something in me that no one else had ever noticed, which in turn gave me the much-needed confidence to follow my dreams. How sad that she couldn't have been a part of my life for just a little longer.

Early in the school year she had assigned a project to be displayed on the large bulletin board at the back of the classroom. She randomly picked myself and one other girl to do the project. I worked like a dog on that assignment, spending day and night for weeks collecting and assembling materials. It was part of our religious education class and we were expected to express, in some sort of a creative way, all the people of the world who were in need of some sort of help, guidance, religion and leadership.

My partner expressed no interest in the project. I came up with the idea to make huge letters from construction paper to spell the word "HELP," followed by a large exclamation point. The corners of the bulletin board were also covered with large triangles to frame the piece. It became a huge collage of pictures of people and animals, any and all who could possibly need help in whatever walk of life they found themselves in. There were many hundreds of pictures ranging from the starving children of Biafra to newlyweds, to doctors and lawyers, obviously starving animals and many other subjects in between. The whole collage covered a space of about 8 × 10 ft. I took hours one night doing the installation alone and I was extremely proud of my work, but nervous, too, that it would not be as good as Sister expected. My partner, Gail, collected dozens of magazines for me, but the idea was all mine. When I finally unveiled the finished project, Sister David actually cried. She was so proud and pleased with my accomplishment. Gail graciously and unselfishly took no credit for the work. Nuns and teachers and even priests were paraded into the classroom for weeks to see my work of art. It was the best feeling ever, even better than coming first. She took pictures of it to send along with my college applications. There were very few times when I've ever felt as proud of myself as I did upon completion of that project.

It was a liberating and joyous experience to be finally understood and to have someone help me on the path to creative endeavours. She encouraged me to apply to the Boston Institute of Design and to Mount St. Vincent University for a degree in fine arts. She helped me with the required submissions for admittance and she was just as elated as I was when I was accepted into both schools. I was not the only one who she helped with their aspirations. She brought in career counsellors and talked to us about the many different paths that were open to us in the future. The pension that I received from the American government, who had employed my father, ensured a fully paid education at the college of my choosing. It was a wonderful legacy.

I saw my boyfriend every weekend and one afternoon a week. Wayne had an aunt and uncle who lived in the city not too far from the hall. I had a standing invitation every Sunday for lunch. Aunt Lucy was a marvellous cook and the table was always laden with golden roasted chickens, roasted meats and every possible accompaniment. After starving all week, I relished every morsel. The large table was always surrounded with noisy but loving family and friends. I told people that I was in love with Wayne and we did have some great times together, but I suspect that I loved Aunt Lucy and her home cooking even more. Whenever I hear that Beatles classic, Hey Jude, I think of those wonderful Sunday afternoons at her home. It was on the hit parade that year and is still one of my all-time favourites. I'll never forget their kindness that year.

Wayne had a motorcycle, which we rode on all year round in all types of weather. He always picked me up at the front door of the hall. One afternoon in the middle of winter, Mother Superior happened to be passing by when he was picking me up. She was appalled that one of her girls was going off with a boy on a motorcycle. How that fact had escaped her for all of the previous months is beyond me. She insisted that my mother be called immediately. I had to call her collect from the payphone in the common room while Mother Superior hovered at my shoulder. My mother, of course, knew that Wayne had a motorcycle and had never had any objections to me riding with him. I suspected that her approval of Wayne was dependant on the fact that his father was a prominent businessman in Gander and had no interest in the fact that he was just a nice guy. Thankfully, she had no objections that day. It was the first and only time that I had ever know Mother

Superior to enter the common room. Wayne was careful to make the loudest getaway possible as we roared down the driveway. It was a satisfying moment.

Sometime shortly after Christmas of that final year, Sister Mary David made it her mission to teach us sex education. It wasn't part of the official curriculum. Up until this point, all we really knew was what we had picked up from each other. Once in a while we were all marched down single file to the audiovisual room to see some lame film presented in animation about how a chicken fertilized an egg. I'm sure, like me, very few of the girls had been given any information at home.

The most that my mother had ever said to me was: "I hope that boy is behaving like a gentleman with you when you go out on dates."

"Of course he is, Mom," would be my reply.

We were all hungry for information. Within a few days, Sister had put a box in the front of the classroom where we could anonymously ask any question that we wanted answered about sex. She promised that nothing was off limits and that she would answer each and every one. She'd only gotten around to answering a few questions before the bottom dropped out of everything. None of the questions were outrageous. Most were just normal teenage curiosity. From what we could piece together, one of the students went home and told her parents what was happening. Sister Mary David vanished from our lives forever. One minute she was there and the next she was gone. She wasn't even given the opportunity to say goodbye. She had been banished, we heard, to some God-forsaken parish in the middle of nowhere. We were all devastated, but probably none more than me.

She was immediately replaced by an insipid, mousey nun whose name I can't even remember. She couldn't hold the attention of a single student and didn't even try to deal with our outrage and rebellion at the loss of Sister Mary David. The rest of the school year went by in a haze. The hours of shift classes were endless. I ended up getting sick with some sort of throat infection that just wouldn't go away. It was further complicated when the doctor gave me penicillin to treat it and I went into anaphylactic shock. I lost all interest in school, in my future and in life in general. I developed migraine headaches that still plague me to this day. I seemed to have a general malaise that never lifted even after my throat infection was finally cleared up. No doubt, my lack of proper nutrition contributed a great deal to all my ailments and to what I now know to be a clinical depression. I still saw my boyfriend regularly, but laughter was elusive. When the time rolled around for the provincial exams, called "CHEs" (Council of Higher Education exams), I couldn't have cared less.

For the first term of that final year, our class had a lay teacher whose husband was employed at the university. She was young, pretty and newly married. She taught us English literature which was my favourite subject. It was obvious within a month or two that she was pregnant. She probably didn't have sufficient money to buy maternity clothes. Tent-like clothing was the accepted norm for pregnant women of the time. We never saw her again after Christmas. She was gone in a poof, just like Sister Mary David, for the sole reason that she was showing a pregnant belly under a regular sweater instead of a voluminous dress. Another victim of the prudishness of the nuns.

Twenty-one

IN JUNE OF THAT FINAL YEAR, THE school put on a luncheon for all graduates. A parent or guardian was invited. We were to wear our graduation gowns. Even the orphans from Belvedere were accompanied by one of the nuns from the convent. To my knowledge, I was the only one there without a parent or older sibling. I don't know if my mother would have come or not. I never invited her.

I did get lucky that year, however, with my roommate. She was a newcomer to the hall. Her name was Linda and she came from the other end of the island and, like me, didn't get to go home very much. We became fast friends. She had an older sister that attended university in the city, also. That was an added bonus. She looked out for us both and was always there for advice if we needed it. It made the year somewhat more bearable. Because of her late arrival to the hall, she was lucky enough to get placed in the early shift classes and was finished every day by 2:30. Our friendship lasted long after our McAuley Hall days, and at one point we ended up living in the same town where our children often played together. We made big plans, Linda and I. We both decided that we would take a gap year, work for a few months, pool our resources and buy a Volkswagen Beetle. We planned to take off in early spring and drive across the country. I guess that in our hearts we knew that it was only a pipe dream, but we wiled away many hours planning for that big trip. After graduation, I didn't run in to Linda again until we found each other standing on the same subway platform in the West End of Toronto. We were both living there at the time. It was a remarkable coincidence. After that, a few more years passed until our next meeting.

A senior class trip was planned for the spring of that year. We were to go to St. Pierre and Miquelon by bus and ferry and spend four days on the islands. It was even more enticing to me than most because French was one of my best subjects. But for me, it was not to be. My stepfather thought that it was a ridiculous idea and wouldn't give me the money to go. I believe it was no more than $100 for the whole trip. My money from my pension would more than cover it. He wouldn't have to spend a dime of his own money to cover the cost. In my house, no meant no. I missed out. Linda went and had a wonderful time. So did everybody who went. I cried for the whole weekend.

I remember so well coming home from school one day to find her in tears after a visit to the eye doctor. This particular ophthalmologist was used by all the girls and nuns of the hall. He was a renowned member of the Catholic community. He was not a young man, perhaps old enough to be our grandfather. I had my eyes checked by him in my junior year and he was well past middle age then. He told her that he would have to examine her and feel her breasts to gauge her level of physical maturity in relationship to her eyes. Not used to questioning a person in authority any more than the rest of us girls, she allowed him to proceed with the examination. He fondled her breasts for quite some time and became visibly aroused. I often wondered how many other unsuspecting girls there were that he tried that same trick on. I always hoped that he would eventually get caught, but I don't think that ever happened. It would have been covered up, no doubt, just as all the other depravities of those years were. Hushed up, as were those crimes of the time committed by the clergy. The police and church worked hand in hand in those days to protect each other.

I had already had my own experiences with sexual predators by this time in my young life. When I was about eleven, I had been fondled and groped by my dentist and attacked by an uncle who was related to me by marriage. In both instances I told my mother, but she didn't believe me either time. She said that I was making it up to get attention. I really didn't even realize what had been done to me, just that it was wrong, and that I had been threatened by harm if I ever told. I learned a valuable lesson, though: I couldn't trust my mother to protect me.

During the winter of my junior year at the hall, a family friend thought that he was doing me a favour by asking his father, who was coming to the city on business, to take me out for a meal. What a treat! Not only was I going out for a fancy dinner, but I was granted permission to go out during the evening hours and on a school night. It was a much-anticipated event, I can tell you that. I had to get all my studying done early. Phone calls were made, permission was given and "Mr. White" picked me up in a taxi at dinner time. I had, of course, known him previously and liked him very much. He took me to the finest place in town, The Newfoundland Hotel, where he was also staying. Dinner was a lavish affair. I wasn't nervous, having been well-trained by the nuns in proper table manners and decorum. I wore my prettiest dress. We were also accompanied by several of his business associates. Mr. White was an older man, again, old enough to be my grandfather. I was treated with much kindness and respect by all of my dining companions. Dinner was served by liveried waiters wearing gloves. It arrived under silver cloches in the finest style.

My curfew was 9 p.m. He asked me to come up to his room with his friends for a while to pass the time before I had to return to the hall. Shortly after arriving in his room, his friends, making a lame and probably prearranged excuse, left us alone. It didn't take him long to make his move. He lifted his chair to face me and was just a hair's breadth away from my face. I could smell the liquor that he had consumed at dinner. I honestly don't know what he could have been thinking, given the fact that we were so closely related by marriage. He actually begged me to have sex with him. At one point he even got down on his knees. I was terrified, of course. I had just turned thirteen years old. He never physically touched me, but the implications were enough to scare me to death. Thoughts flew through my head. How was I going to get out of this mess? Did I have some kind of sign on my forehead that made all old men think that I was easy prey? Would he force me to have sex with him? Would it hurt a lot? Who would ever believe me if I decided to tell? Would I bleed? Can I run faster than him? If I ran, would I make the long walk home in time for curfew?

When his begging got him nowhere, and after I tearfully pleaded with him to take me back to the hall, he offered me a very large sum of money to have sex with him. Of course, he failed at this as well. In the end, all he did was to plead with me not to tell his son or daughter-in-law what he'd done. He wouldn't let me leave until I made him that promise. He finally sent me home alone in a taxi. I didn't tell anyone about the incident for a very long time. A few years later I did tell my mother, when I heard that we were going to drop in and visit him and his wife while we were on a road trip. Once again, she didn't believe. A nice man like Mr. White could not possibly be responsible for such terrible actions. I was attention-seeking once again, she said. I never confided in her about anything, not ever again. The pattern had been going on for all of my young life. If ever I informed her of anybody's wrongdoing, she blamed me. I suppose, for her, it was easier than dealing with the realities of some of the situations that I found myself in.

After shaking off my goody two shoes, I managed to find my share of trouble during those years at the hall. I gossiped right along with the other girls. It was a common practice at the hall. I told white lies but made sure that I was absolved of all my sins every Saturday morning in the confessional box. Perhaps my biggest transgressions were my efforts to gain attention from anybody and everybody. This was not surprising, given the fact that I was literally starving for it at home.

In my grade 10 class there was a girl who had epilepsy. She was hovered over and received more attention than any other student. I hatched a plan one night during study period and decided that I was going to fake a seizure. What better way to get every girl in the hall and all the nuns to come running? I hadn't figured out how to foam at the mouth, but I was determined to give it my best shot. A bit of drooling should do the trick. My performance, so I thought, was Oscar-worthy. Everyone did come running. Nuns flocked to my bedside and stayed there for hours, soothing my brow, pencils at the ready to stick in my mouth so that I didn't swallow my tongue. Girls twittered away up and down the corridors. Sister Elaine, our nurse, was out somewhere that evening but as soon as she returned she hurried to my bedside. It didn't take her long to realize that there had been no seizure, no bump on my head from my sudden fall to the floor and, in fact, no ill effects at all. My roommate was thoroughly questioned and broke her silence pretty quickly. I was confined to my room for a week, but the embarrassment alone was enough punishment. I was watched carefully for a while, which had been part of my plan from the start. Attention was attention, however I could come by it. Before too long, things went back to normal.

Twenty-two

AFTER MY HEARTBREAK AND THE SUBSEQUENT FALSE allegations of theft by my roommate, Mary Ellen, I went through a pretty low period, which I already told you about. One sleepless night I decided that life was no longer worth living. I took an overdose of about twenty Contac-C capsules, a popular cold remedy at the time. My head swirled through a sea of stars before I fell off to sleep. To this day, I'm unable to tell you whether or not I really wanted to kill myself or just get to a temporary place of peace and oblivion. Lack of sleep does terrible things to the mind and body and I hadn't had a good night's sleep in at least a month. I was awakened, as usual, in the morning by Sister Elaine when she did the bed checks. I had the most horrendous headache and confessed to her what I'd done. She didn't believe that I'd tried to take my own life. After all, what young girl would risk eternal damnation in hell. A phone call was placed to my mother, and before the end of the day I found myself in a psychiatrist's office. I refused to utter a word throughout the entire appointment, and after the hour was up I was finally released from his smoke-filled office. I was put in a taxi and back to the hall. The irony of the story is that the psychiatrist shot himself in the head before I had a chance to return for my next appointment. Perhaps he had been diagnosed with a terminal illness. Who knows? The incident was never mentioned again, either by my mother or the nuns.

I often, especially in my first year, told lies, mostly exaggerations about my home life, all in an effort to get people to pity me. I probably didn't need to exaggerate at all. The reality was bad enough. I told about regular beatings from my stepfather. In truth, he had beaten me, but not as much as my mother did. He was, of course, bigger and stronger, and when he hit me it wasn't uncommon for me to fly across the room. It didn't happen often, but when it did I laid low for weeks or months.

During that second year I made friends outside the hall, girls in my class, mostly, who in turn would introduce me to others. I was a bit of a curiosity, because I lived at the hall. Some wanted me to sneak them in to have a look at the place, but I never had enough nerve for that. It was in this way that I came to know Patricia and Sara. They were best friends and had been for all of their lives. They were endlessly curious about the strange world in which I lived. They both came from large families. Towards the end of the school year, I was invited to dinner at their homes and asked to go on a weekend outing for the 24th of May weekend. It wasn't until I got to the cabin that I realized that there would be no adult supervision. The fact would probably not have made much difference to me anyway. I was up for some adventure. Patricia's older sister was the closest that we had to a chaperone and I don't think that she was more than seventeen. I was becoming more and more fascinated by how the other half lived.

The first sign of trouble started on the morning of our arrival. I had asked and been given permission to visit the family for the weekend and, of course, the nuns had no idea of the circumstances of my visit. They thought that I was in safe hands. We were sent to the grocery store to buy supplies for the weekend. Wieners and marshmallows were a must for the campfire. This little taste of freedom was going to be delicious; freedom from the nuns, no adults, no stepfather and lots of junk food and late nights.

As usual I had no money but was assured that I didn't need any. I was, after all, their guest. So off we went, Patricia, Sara and myself. When we got to the store we started picking out our supplies. The girls were gathering T-bone steaks and all kinds of other expensive goodies. Then they told me that they didn't have any money either. We were meant to shoplift everything and make a speedy getaway. Up until this point in my life I had stolen nothing more than a single cigarette from my stepfather to smoke in the woods across the street from our house. This new adventure was shockingly dangerous, but thrilling as well. I hesitated but a moment before fleeing from the scene with all those tasty foodstuffs hidden under our jackets. Upon arriving back at the cabin, we were applauded by Patricia's older sister and her friends. I'm ashamed to say that it was not my last act of theft while hanging around with those girls. Under Patricia's sister's tutelage, they were all experts and I was an apt pupil. We never got caught but I lived in fear of the moment when the police would come to the doors of the hall and take me away to jail. I remember playing some sort of game that weekend that involved a broom and twirling around in a circle until we passed out. Some of the girls fainted, but I never did. It was probably dangerous. Everything that they did was dangerous.

I was afraid, yes, but it was a thrilling ride while it lasted. I was glad when the school year came to an end, glad that I was getting away from those girls. The stress had become too much, and I couldn't live with my guilty conscience. I thought that my criminal past was done and over with it but there was more to come, this time in the form of aiding and abetting. I didn't dare confess my sins to Father Eastman, but instead walked to the basilica on Saturday afternoons. I was fearful that he would recognize my voice.

One day in July of that summer, a knock came on the door of my house in Gander. On the other side stood Patricia. She had decided to come for a week's vacation and we were to be the lucky hosts. I may have invited her in passing, but no firm plans were ever made, and she didn't warn me of her visit. My mother was at home when she arrived and had little choice but to let her stay. Keep in mind that they had never even met before, nor had I ever mentioned any sort of visit. She knew that I'd spent a weekend with her family and, I suppose, felt obliged to return the favour. Patricia had travelled by train to Gander and we were stuck with her.

From the moment that she arrived she wanted to know where the best places were to shoplift, where she could meet boys and where she could sell some of the things that she stole. I didn't know any of the answers to her questions. I lived a crime-free life in Gander and wanted it to stay that way. I quickly realized that I was in way over my head. She had to share my bed in the basement and on that first night she furtively slipped out of the window above the washing machine and didn't return until the early hours of the following morning. I was terrified. If she was caught, then I would be guilty by association and probably exiled to Belvedere Orphanage. She spent the rest of the week shoplifting wherever and whenever she could.

In order to explain away her new belongings and the gifts that she "bought" for her family we had to lie to my mother, who was obviously curious. She told Mom that she'd gone to bingo before leaving home and was lucky enough to win $500. That was a lot of money in 1968. So, lies piled upon more lies. When she returned home, she told her mother that she'd gone to bingo in Gander and won the money there. I was, of course, sworn to secrecy. By this time, I knew that I was involved with a true juvenile delinquent, or perhaps a whole family of them.

The only roadblock keeping me from having any more to do with Patricia was her best friend, Sara. She wanted me to come and stay with her and her family. Sara was the follower of the two and getting away from my home in Gander was always a welcome prospect. After promises were made that we wouldn't be spending any time with Patricia, I finally agreed. Her mother wrote to mine and the plan was put into place. Sara's family was nice, and she had a lovely mom who cooked me all my favourite meals. She knew how horrible the food was at the hall and seemed to disagree, in general, with my family's decision to send me there at all. When I got to Sara's, I told her that there would be no more stealing or trouble-making. My brief life as an outlaw was over. She agreed. I don't think that she wanted to be involved in those activities any more than I did. We talked a lot about the terrible things that we'd done during the last few months of school while I was staying with Patricia. My guilt, though more overwhelming then hers, had taken its toll. I like to think that I may have turned her away from the dark side, just a little.

While staying with them, Sara's older brother developed a bit of a crush on me. He was nice, but I wasn't really interested. He was a little too old for me and I was reluctant to get involved with anybody like that. I'd learned my lesson with Edward. On my last night there, and after much encouragement from his family, I agreed to go out with him to visit some of his friends. It wasn't really a formal date, so I figured that I'd be safe enough. He had planned on taking me to meet a friend of his and his wife who had just recently had a baby. This in itself was a draw. I'd never met or even knew of any teenagers who had a baby, let alone a couple who had dropped out of school and gotten married because of it. Sara's brother was a true gentleman, and all went well until we arrived at his friend's apartment.

That visit was a real eye opener for the both of us. It was a cold and foggy summer evening, so typical of a St. John's night, even in summer. The poor couple didn't even have windows, just some plastic taped in a few spots for protection from the rain. They lived in a third-floor tenement in the poorest part of the city. They may as well have lived on the streets. It was my first experience with true poverty. They had no running water, lamps that were lit by kerosene oil and no toilet facilities except for a communal toilet down the hall. Their obvious pain and embarrassment at their living conditions was awful to witness. Sara's brother was in shock, as well. If ever there was a walking, talking advertisement for abstinence, then they were it. Their poor little baby screamed for the entire time that we stayed, no doubt it was half starved. The whole experience left us dumbfounded. If I'd had any money at all I would have left it behind. Sara's brother dropped a $5 bill on the table as we left. I thought of that poor family for a long time afterwards and often wondered if they ever managed to climb out of that situation. Apparently, she was Catholic and he wasn't. That combined with the sin of her pregnancy had been enough for both their parents to cut them out of their lives entirely. I don't even know if social assistance was available back then. I think they were afraid to ask for help for fear of losing their baby. They were barely out of childhood themselves.

Sometime in the late spring of that same year, just after the weekend at the cabin, I was invited to spend a Sunday afternoon with Patricia's grandfather and the rest of the family at a cabin somewhere up on the South Side Hills behind Fort Amherst. Fort Amherst is the location of the lighthouse that guides ships in and out of the narrow entrance to St. John's Harbour. Anyone who is at all familiar with the city will realize that back then it was a pretty remote location. It probably still is.

One of Patricia's brothers rowed us across the harbour and then we had a steep and lengthy climb up the hills to the cabin that was located in the woods at the top. It was a gruelling journey. When we finally arrived, we were met with a lot of grownups who had obviously been drinking heavily. I wondered, once again, how I kept getting myself into these situations. We stayed for a while, but the trek had taken up much of the afternoon. I was in a dilemma. The worst possible outcome was obvious. How was I going to get back to the hall before curfew? I would be denied privileges for a week or more, no doubt about it. There must have been some sort of back road that had brought all those fat old men to the cabin, but no one was willing to take me home. After much pleading, I was offered the use of the rowboat to get back across the harbour. My so-called friend wouldn't leave, so I set off on my own. I flew down the cliffs, feet barely making contact with the ground, never really knowing if I was heading towards the harbour or straight into the North Atlantic. I did eventually make it down, climbed aboard the little boat and rowed like a maniac back across the harbour.

I was driven by pure fear. I really didn't think that I could make it, but I did. An Olympic rower would not have been able to match my speed that afternoon. Upon reaching the docks on the city side of the harbour, a kind sailor who had been watching my progress with great interest helped me to tie up the rowboat. I remember thinking afterwards that it had probably been stolen. I still had the arduous climb up Garrison Hill ahead of me. I wish I could say that I made it back in time for curfew, but I was at least an hour late. Grounded for a week was the outcome of that afternoon. It's an afternoon that I'll never forget. When I get the opportunity now to look out over the harbour, I'm truly amazed that one day, many, many years ago, I actually rowed across it in a little boat, all by myself.

There's no doubt that I learned a lot of lessons from the time spent with Sara, Patricia and their families. I never saw them much during my final year except in passing once in a while in the corridors at school. I kept a wide berth whenever possible. I wouldn't be at all surprised to know that Patricia continued on with her criminal ways. It would be interesting to know what paths their lives have taken.

Twenty-three

IT IS NO EXAGGERATION TO SAY THAT I never was much of an athlete. I hate sports of all kinds, whether it be participating or watching. Physical education was a big part of our school curriculum. We had classes twice weekly and if at all possible I skipped. In the early days I really did try to make an effort, and even joined a volleyball team. I lasted through about fifteen minutes of one game. My main incentive in joining the team was the fact that it was coached by one of the nuns. We all wanted to take in the sight of her jumping around in her constricting habit. She put on sneakers for the game, tied her veil back in an elastic and somehow pinned up the bottom of her flowing skirts so that we could actually see her ankles. She obviously loved the physical activities and had probably been a great athlete in her younger days. I soon grew tired of that particular novelty and set about developing the fine art of skipping gym class. I faced a lot of road blocks. We had a lay teacher for the second and third year, and after a while she just gave up on me. There were, by then, too many students to control, and the loss of little old me wasn't of much consequence to her. I hated the communal showers and the echoes in the gymnasium every time somebody scored a goal, but most of all I hated getting sweaty and I hated the smell of everyone else's sweat. I got enough of that at the hall. In general, the nuns did not adhere much to the "healthy mind, healthy body" philosophy.

I did join in a few extracurricular activities. For about a year I played drums in the high school band and attended choir practice regularly. I had a decent singing voice, but my percussion's, well ... not so great. I got some pretty dark looks from the band director when I felt compelled to go a little heavy on the bass. We were told that belonging to school programs would look good on a college application, so I decided to join a group who was starting up a school newspaper. The adventure failed miserably. Our first publication had a controversial article, the subject of which I no longer remember. The first edition became the last.

Living with the nuns under such strict rules and guidelines made me into a person who was finely skilled in the art of deception. None of us ever thought of it as a bad thing. It became our way of life, our mission, if you will, and more than anything a habit to do anything and everything to avoid following the rules. We almost always lied about our whereabouts, covered for each other when needed, helped others to keep out of trouble and to cause as much mayhem as possible without getting caught. The very way in which we were forced to live seemed to demand it. I don't know of a single girl who did not act out, even in a minor way, at one time or another.

In my final year, when we were allowed more privileges, we often lied about where we were going. A high school dance was always allowed but some of the places that my boyfriend and I went were definitely off limits. We went to a Turtles concert one night, university dances, spent time alone in his room at his residence at the university, went for long rides into the country on his motorcycle, went for long drives in his uncle's car where we usually ended up parking, and committed many other acts of defiance.

The only way that we could actually get permission to go anywhere in the evening was if we approached the Dean of Girls and pled our case. If we were forceful enough to convince her that there was safety in numbers, then a rare exception would be made.

Those were the circumstances that brought us to the Old Colony Club, a St. John's institution that acted as a nightclub, banquet hall, restaurant and—on that particular night—the location for a teenage dance. It was a dance that was not sponsored by the church or any of the schools, so it was amazing that we were allowed to go at all. A lot of the senior girls were in attendance, along with myself, my roommate Linda and our respective boyfriends. Linda and I were a little shocked by the behaviour of some of our hall-mates that night. Not only were there a lot of public displays of affection going on with boys that we didn't know, but there was also a substantial amount of drinking taking place. The girls were known to me, of course. Two of them actually had a room next to mine. I didn't hang around with them much, so I was pretty shocked to see that they had taken their own liquor to the dance and were liberally consuming it.

It wasn't until years later that I found out that several of the girls at the hall were drinking on a regular basis. Apparently, they would hide their booze in the basement in unused lockers and consume it there as well. If the liquor was discovered, then no one would be found guilty. The nuns would have no idea who it belonged to. During a television interview, long after we'd all entered adulthood, one of the girls talked about how her year at the hall had begun her downward slide into teenage alcoholism. I probably would have forgotten about that dance at the Old Colony Club had it not been for that interview. It opened my eyes to a whole other side of life at the hall, one that I never even knew existed. It made some of our stolen smokes in the bathtub room and other shenanigans seem mild in comparison. Lots of girls were apparently drinking on a regular basis. I saw none of it, however, even though it was going on right under my nose. Would I have joined in had I known? Probably not.

Drugs and alcohol never did hold much of an allure for me. Somehow it made all our transgressions seem mild in comparison. After that night at the Old Colony Club my roommate and I kept mostly to ourselves and continued to double date. I had introduced her to my boyfriend's best friend and by then they had become an item. When I wasn't with my boyfriend, I spent a lot of time at Memorial University Library pretending to study. We had a perfectly good library at Holy Heart, but I just wanted to be as far away from the hall as I possibly could.

The biggest event of the high school year was the Winter Carnival Dance. We had no official graduation prom. Instead, the prom and graduation ceremonies were always held the following December, six months after we had left school. It was an odd practice, but the nuns felt that if a girl did not pass, then she was not entitled to a formal celebration. By the following year, most students had moved on, whether to universities out of the province or to Toronto to find work.

The Winter Carnival Dance was a much-anticipated event. Linda and I were picked up by our respective boyfriends in a car that Wayne had borrowed from his uncle for the evening. I wore the same lovely dress that had been made the year before for my New Year's with Steve. The nuns took in the event from a vantage point, high above the gymnasium.

Linda's boyfriend had somehow acquired two bottles of beer and the two boys drank it in the car before we went inside. I was upset, felt that we were flirting with danger, and Linda and I were both terrified that we would be caught. We had been given endless warnings about what would happen if any one of those attending stepped out of line. We weren't allowed to leave the building nor enter other parts of the school and were not allowed to go anywhere that might lead us into the path of temptation. The nuns patrolled the parking lot at regular intervals, searching for steamy windows or couples who were in each other's arms.

Two beers seem so harmless now, but back then it put the fear of God in us. Thankfully, the boys were never caught and we had a wonderful evening. The lights were never dimmed, not even for the last waltz. I still have pictures of that evening in that brightly lit gymnasium. The nuns were adamant that no girl would lose her virtue that evening under their collective watch.

Even though I did not pass my final exams, I was given the opportunity to write substitute exams in Gander later that summer. I failed two of my subjects that final year, French and math. I had excelled at French all throughout high school and had always had a gift for languages, and I studied Spanish as well. I guess it just goes to show how uninterested I was in the outcome of that final year. I had well and truly given up. I passed the substitute exams with flying colours, giving me graduation marks with honours. I didn't much care. I wanted no accolades, had given up on the idea of either of the schools that had accepted me, lost my deposits and moved on.

I had told my mother that I was not going to pass. I hadn't even bothered to finish writing my math test. She didn't seem to take me seriously until the final marks came in the mail at the end of July. The events following that report card made the rest of my summer a misery. I had picked up a part-time job, but she wouldn't let me work, thinking that I would get up to evil ways if I had some extra money in my pocket. So, there I was, finished high school and still living on $5 a week. By that fall I had found another job and worked at it until I had saved enough money to get to Toronto. Back then, Toronto was the desired destination for most young Newfoundlanders and the one place where we thought that we would find the pot of gold at the end of the rainbow. It was no hardship to leave. After all, I was living in a boarding house. Without anyone to guide me, I thought that it was the best choice. I didn't even bother to say goodbye to my family. When I thought that I'd saved enough money to survive in the big city, I just packed a few things and left.

I had no interest in going to my graduation ceremonies in December and no interest in revisiting my past or the people who had been a part of it.

Twenty-four

WHEN A PERSON IS EDUCATED BY NUNS, they learn early on how to be silent. Our school, with upwards of two thousand students, was a remarkably quiet environment. We weren't allowed to raise our voices for any reason, nor run or behave in any way that could be construed as a boisterous manner. We always had to walk in a single file to the right in the corridors or stairways. To behave in any other way meant a trip to the principal's office, or to the Dean of Discipline. Neither of those fates was desirable. Strangely enough, other things that should have been a matter of course in a large school were left neglected. I don't remember ever being encouraged to wash our hands before meals or after using the washroom. As I've mentioned, some of the girls at the hall had a terrible problem with body odour; they never showered, washed their hair or tended to any other basic feminine needs in a hygienic manner. It was not unusual to see a used sanitary napkin sitting on a girl's bed or to see soiled panties left in plain sight. Presumably, Sister Elaine had to speak to those girls to set them on the right track. We often had to hold our noses while walking by some of the girl's rooms.

Some girls had terrible table manners when they first arrived at the hall. Some used their fingers to eat instead of using utensils and chewed large amounts of food with their mouths open. It made for some very uncomfortable meals and one of the reasons that I often sat alone or avoided certain tables. The nuns would give us periodic lessons on the subject, but usually the worst culprits never thought that the lectures were directed at them.

I didn't have too many body issues back then, at least no more than any other average teenage girl experiences. I've told you about some of the episodes where I acted out, and of my small acts of rebellion and other acts of criminal behaviour. I was certainly not the worse of the bunch, but I believe that because I could never get away with even the smallest act of misbehaviour at home, I only did as much as I felt that I could get away with. I look around now, at this point in my life, at people who have come through childhood trauma such as mine, and I realize that I could have ended up in a very different place. Lots ended up on a road to self-destruction, from where there was no return. I feel very lucky to be where I am today.

All this brings me to my most private and destructive phase. It started in grade 9 and went on during most of my years at the hall. It was something that I struggled with, even afterwards, during periods of high anxiety or stress. I pulled out my hair. There is a condition called trichotillomania, characterized as an impulse control disorder and often triggered in childhood by high levels of anxiety. It most often occurs in young girls. I was deeply ashamed of my habit, but for me it was a way of making myself feel better, and in some strange way it offered me comfort. The disorder is often treated with cognitive behaviour therapy and drugs. There is debate amongst the medical community nowadays as to whether anxiety is a direct result of the hair pulling or whether the hair pulling becomes the disorder. It is most often caused by depression and high stress situations. My mother noticed my hair pulling. One could not help but notice that I no longer had eyelashes or eyebrows and had huge bald spots on my head. She just used to tell me to take my hands away from my hair. My friends noticed my lack of eyelashes. I would just lie and say that I'd pulled them out by accident with an eyelash curler.

With my new awareness and growing maturity, I saw my own world changing drastically. I didn't know how to cope with these new feelings of mine and had no one to guide me along the way. I kept my hair pulling a secret as much as I could.

I learned how to wear my hair in new ways to cover the bald spots. Before too long the problem was out of control. The nuns, of course, never noticed. Soon one side of my head was almost completely bald. I kept my hair long, so I could pull it to one side. Before long I also began to create sores on my arms and legs where no one else could see. I was a mess. I thought that I was the only person in the world who was engaging in such an activity. It frightened me a lot. Sometimes, I would get myself under control enough to let my eyebrows grow back, but the compulsion was powerful. I was well and truly addicted to the behaviour. Once day, in the same way that I gave up smoking years later, I decided that enough was enough. Without treatment of any kind I quit, just like that.

By final year, it was obvious that the glory days of the hall were coming to an end. Numbers were down, and girls were being taken in on a short-term basis just to study for exams. When the numbers went down, so did the quality and quantity of the food. It went from bad to worse. I barely ate a meal in the cafeteria, often not eating more than a cold tin of soup once a week. I waited with great anticipation for the weekends and the wonderful meals at Wayne's aunt's house. It's no wonder that I had a throat infection that wouldn't go away.

The hair pulling and sores on my legs didn't hurt. By grade 11, I'd developed another destructive habit, brought about, no doubt, by my lack of nutrition. I developed sores under my nails. The skin would actually pull away from the nail bed causing bleeding and scabbing. It's one of the early signs of scurvy, and no doubt my lack of vitamin C was the root cause. All those tiny nerve endings at my fingertips would scream. I would lie in bed at night and cry from the pain. I had an old pair of white cotton gloves leftover from my confirmation that I started wearing to bed after covering my fingers with Ozonol, a frequently used antibiotic ointment of the time. It worked a little, but they never did get better, not until I left the hall and started to eat a proper diet. Even today, when I'm stressed I play with my hair, but I refrain from the hair pulling. In grade 12, after Sister Mary David left, I wiled away my classroom hours by braiding and unbraiding tiny sections of my hair.

When picking the sores on my arms and legs weren't enough to satisfy me, I began punching myself hard enough to cause huge bruises. The bigger and blacker the bruise got, the better I felt. If I'd had access to a sharp object I probably would have been cutting myself, as well.

Twenty-five

BY THE TIME THAT I GOT BACK to the hall after that first Christmas at home and announced to my mother that I was going to join the convent, I thought that my path was laid out before me in the form of a joyous service to God. Shortly after seeing the true colours of the nuns, that calling disappeared. Although some, I'm sure, had a true calling to serve the Lord and to serve the children in their charge, most were very narcissistic, and never bothered to hide the fact. But that, I suppose, is the very nature of a narcissist. They never see themselves as one. When a person goes through a large part of their life on a pedestal being revered and adored, as these people were, I suppose it's easy to see how they lost the true motives that called them to that way of life in the first place.

That kind of power—in some, at least—brings about the abuse of that power. All of our eyes were opened that first year.

These so-called saintly women used and abused their power often and seemingly without regret. Pride, we were taught, was the most dangerous sin of all and could lead to the downfall of many a good person. "Love yourself first," was a mantra that they discouraged at every level. Self-confidence and pride in one's achievements was something that they discouraged at every turn, yet we saw their arrogance constantly. With our growing maturity, we began to see these Godly women in a clearer light. It was very disconcerting to have one's belief system blown to bits.

With my new awareness and growing maturity, I saw my own world change drastically. I didn't know how to cope with these new realities. Perhaps that's why I turned to those self-destructive habits.

The kidnapping of the mind that the Catholic Church engaged in back in those days began from the moment that we entered school and was hard to break away from. The cult-like atmosphere of the church back then was hard to shake and had a powerful hold on us all.

I really don't know why I became more jaded than others. A lot of girls remained strong in their faith, but then a lot of them had not been a resident of the hall for a full three years. By grade 11, I was no longer a regular sight at morning Mass. I often went to the hall chapel after study period, not for comfort and prayer, but because it was a quiet, dark and empty place, a place where I could shed my tears in private.

Privacy was a rare commodity at the hall. Even the girls wishing to spend time with their boyfriends were often spied upon. I'm not sure if I'm a private person by nature, or if the hall made me that way. Most, by now, would say after reading this book that I'm not very private at all. I'm never happier then when my house is empty and I can relish the silence around me. I've told my family many times that if I have to be put in a home in my waning years then please make sure that I don't have a roommate. I've had enough of those to last me a lifetime.

I joined the few girls that took baths in the afternoon and would soak in bubbles in that tiny closet of a room for hours on end. Most hours of the day our doors were required to be open. If found closed, some nun, without even knocking, would promptly open them. Invariably, there were always a few snorers. It was not always easy to get a good night's sleep.

We had a large storage room in the basement where our trunks were stored. I would often get permission to go down there just to get away from everybody. We alternated clothes from season to season and I used this excuse to go there at least once a week. It was in an isolated part of the basement near the laundry room and both rooms were always deserted at night. Trunks were stacked from floor to ceiling and my own became a large treasure chest. I had taken pictures from home of my father and poured over them endlessly, imagining that somewhere out there he was still alive and would walk back into my life at any moment. I looked for him on every street corner for every one of those years. I wasn't delusional. I had actually seen his body in the coffin. I don't think that I was acting much differently than any child who loses a parent at an early age.

That final year, I started going to visit his grave at Belvedere Cemetery, which was just a short walk away from the hall. I spent hours there in the fine weather with him, and then afterwards walking around and studying the ancient tombstones. My grandfather, Skippy, was buried in the same plot as my father. He lived with us until he died when I was ten years old. I mourned him as much as I did my father. Right after Skippy's death, my mother remarried. I suppose it was a pretty morose pastime for a young girl.

Twenty-six

SOMETIME DURING THE WINTER OF THAT FINAL year, I was invited to try out for the title of Miss Teen Newfoundland. It began after I was spotted by one of the organizers at some school event or another. The next step was an intense interview. I was asked during the interview what my favourite pastime was. I told them, honestly enough, that visiting graveyards was something that I loved to do. I was positive that this would make me a suitable candidate for the finals. I can just imagine the thoughts that went through the minds of the panel. What if I was lucky enough to win and was asked, on a national stage, the same question? Figure skating or singing, or even reading would obviously have made me more suitable. But, of course, I wanted to come off as interesting and unique. When asked what my future plans were, I replied that I wanted to be a speech pathologist. What in God's name had I been thinking? I have no idea what hat I pulled that answer from. I didn't even know what a speech pathologist was. I'd seen the occupation on some brochure at school and supposed that it made me sound smart. I don't know why I didn't tell them that I wanted to become a designer and had been accepted into two prestigious schools for that very career.

After Sister Mary David left, I lost confidence in my creative abilities. I had no idea how a speech pathologist became a speech pathologist or even if it required a university education. I just thought that it made me sound kind of smart. I was then asked why I had chosen this particular career path. An answer was not forthcoming. My aspirations of becoming Miss Teen World were over, right there and then. I got to the final twelve in the local pageant and that was the end of that. Unfortunately, some of the girls at the hall found out about my audition and I became the victim of a lot of teasing and ridicule. This failure came on the heels of my try-out for the cheerleading squad, another disaster in a series of disasters. At that time, I was again asked to join the group and made it to the final cut, this, I suspect, was mostly due to my height. Those cheerleaders were the "it" girls, and I desperately wanted to be a part of them. My lack of physical aptitude and absence at any gym class over the years came back to haunt me. I couldn't even kick my legs up past my waist. All those ballet exercises couldn't even help me. Most of the girls could kiss their knees, but not me. My attempts were pathetic. I was cut in the first half hour, another humiliation that I had to suffer. I was failing at every turn. I couldn't seem to shake the cloud that was hanging over me for most of that final year.

I still managed to have some fun, though. The sadder I was, the funnier I tried to be. The older girls enjoyed having me around. Watched less closely than ever before, I was always game for a prank or some sort of mischief. We used to do something called French-bedding. It was a lot of work and meant making lots of beds. Basically, it meant re-making a girl's bed very precisely so that when she turned down her covers at night her feet would go no farther than halfway down the bed. We usually put the plan into motion during the supper hour. Since I rarely went near the cafeteria anymore this became our prime time. It was funny, but very frustrating for the girls who wanted nothing more than an early night. The worst part for the victim was that she'd have to get up and start from scratch to remake her bed. There was no other way around it. We'd stand close, giggling and waiting for the moment when she would climb into her bed, listening for the inevitable cries of frustration. We spent many hours substituting sugar for salt in their respective containers, hiding pyjamas, pouring coloured water into shampoo and any other silliness that we could think of.

Twenty-seven

HOME ECONOMICS WAS ANOTHER REQUIRED SUBJECT AT school. We were taught what was then referred to as the "domestic sciences." Cooking, sewing, how to properly make a bed, budgeting, shopping and how to properly clean a house were all part of the package. Sister Mary Angela was our teacher. She was quite elderly, but very patient. I excelled at bed making, of course, did a decent job of cooking, but dressmaking skills were beyond me. I hated using the sewing machine and still do, but she found that I had a real gift for hand stitching. I hated the precision and patience required to fiddle with the huge machines, threading them and oiling them was beyond me. She was amazed then that I had the gift for hand stitching, and often took me over to the school in the evenings and on Sunday mornings to teach me the finer stitches required for ribbon embroidery, a hobby that I still love. The only downside to her attentions was that I would often miss an evening phone call from my boyfriend.

Our common areas at the hall consisted of two rooms and a vestibule. The vestibule was furnished with our wooden phone booth, which had a door and three sides of windows at the top and a few uncomfortable chairs to sit in while we waited for a call. Usually, while waiting for a call we sat on the tiled floor. The phone booth was the only purpose of that particular room. During our senior year the nuns had a pop machine installed for us. It dispensed white paper cups that filled with cola for ten cents. It was a wonderful addition to our lives. I always managed to save a few dimes for the treat. On occasion, the machine would have some kind of meltdown and fill cups over and over again without our ever having to insert any coins. We all lived for those blips in the machinery. Free pop for all. After those episodes, the machine would generally be out of order or empty for a week or two. It's hard to describe the joy felt when a glass-full of that glorious, dark liquid came pouring out.

There was a small common room just off the vestibule that housed a TV and a ping-pong table. The ping-pong table was always in use during free time. Some girls were addicted to the game and had raucous competitions. I may have played once or twice, but that was about it. The television only received one channel: the CBC. I only remember watching television twice over that three-year period. The first time was when Pierre Elliot Trudeau became leader of the Liberal Party in March of 1968, and again in April of that same year when he was elected prime minister. Sister Mary Margaret had turned me on to his charms and she was a great supporter of his, and then, of course, in turn, so was I. She even managed to find and gift me with an autographed picture of him. For many years it was one of my most prized possessions. I adored everything about him, first of all because she did, and then later on because of his own merits.

The television was watched by a devoted few. I have no idea what they watched. I remember looking in many times to see girls staring glassy-eyed at the screen. We weren't allowed up late enough to watch the news. For those years, the small screen could never hold my interest. I was usually too busy waiting for a phone call.

The larger common room was a quieter room furnished with some old books and some older but comfy squishy furniture. It had windows that looked out onto the driveway and on weekends was always occupied by girls waiting for the boyfriends or families to arrive. It also had a set of those same garage-like doors that were in the kitchen. There were a few appliances behind them, but the only time in my memory that the room was ever used was when we had that Halloween party back in junior year. There was a long dark corridor that ran along the side where Sister Mary Therese took us girls for our private talks. It was also used sometimes by other nuns when one or another of us was getting a private scolding.

Most of the girls went home for weekends by taxi that took them to their homes or the coastal boats, or they were picked up by their parents. We were always curious to see what the fathers and mothers of the girls looked like, so the room was almost always occupied and fairly quiet.

My home town was about four and a half hours away by car. Gander was an airport town, and so with a student pass I often flew home for the grand total of $11. I didn't go home often, but when I did my mother would pay the fare in advance in Gander and my uncle would drive me to the airport to take a Friday evening flight.

It was Christmas vacation of my final year. Holding a student pass meant that I was always on standby. I had always made it onto the flights except for that particular night. I didn't even have a dime on me to use the pay phone to call my uncle to come back for me when I didn't make it onto the flight. Broke as usual. Back in those days, after the last flight left the airport was closed. The security guard had no choice but to lock me in the airport for the night. I asked him if he would give me a dime for the payphone, but he refused. I could have been more insistent, but I was afraid to have too much conversation with an older man. I had learned my lesson the hard way and stayed as far away from older men as I could. I had to sleep in the airport all alone that night without food or water or any comforts. I spent most of my time in the ladies' washroom, thinking that I would be safest there. I was too scared to sleep much. After finally arriving in Gander the following morning, I called my mother to come and get me. She had presumed that I'd spent the night at my aunt and uncle's house and couldn't understand why I didn't get a taxi back to the hall. If I didn't have the money for a phone call, then I certainly didn't have the money for a taxi. She gave me a lecture on the virtues of having some money put aside for just such an emergency. What money? She was clueless. I'm sure if I'd called the nuns they would not have seen me stranded, but it was another ten cents that I didn't have. I was still a child being forced to think and act like an adult. I did try to do just that most of the time, but sometimes I just got so tired of being responsible and therefore made some poor choices.

Twenty-eight

IN CASE YOU THINK THAT I LEFT my life of crime behind a little too easily, I might as well tell you about the event that precipitated my fall from grace in the first place. Up until now, I've been blaming Patricia for leading me down that path. Nothing could be further from the truth. I wasn't sure if I wanted to talk about the following events, but perhaps it will give you a better understanding of my drastic and downward spiral in grade 10. It wasn't just because of my heartbreak over Steve or my troubles with Mary Ellen.

My mother and stepfather came to pick me up that year to take me home for Easter vacation. We went to Bowrings for lunch, as was our usual habit, and then we went shopping. Shopping was the only mother-daughter time that we ever had together. We were making the rounds of the department stores as usual, ending the afternoon at the Royal Stores. I have no idea where my stepfather was. My mother had a distant cousin who worked at the store and we always stopped to have a chat with him. It was during this chat while she was browsing through a rack of skirts that I saw a sight that has stayed with me to this day. I watched as my mother shoplifted two skirts, all the while talking to her cousin who was standing just a few racks away. There are really and truly no words to describe the feelings that went through my heart and soul that day. I had been brought up to be a good Catholic girl and my mother, although not the most devout of all the mothers that I knew, never missed Sunday mass or confession on Saturday afternoons or all the rituals of Lent and Advent. Her mother, in turn, was the holiest of women and often referred to by my mother as a saint. It was as if I was in some crazy dream and couldn't wake up. I knew, though, that my eyes had not deceived me.

We were to spend that night at my step-grandfather's house in Bay Roberts before returning to Gander for all the rituals of Good Friday. Good Friday was and is the most important day of the Roman Catholic's liturgical calendar. It meant making the Stations of The Cross three times with prolonged prayers at each station. This was followed by an even longer service, in which the priest prostrated himself on the altar. Then came the ritual of the washing of the feet, likened to the washing of the feet performed upon Christ by Mary Magdalene. There was then a general absolution of all our sins, followed finally by the most sacred Mass of the year.

I had a lot of time to think during that night and on the long drive back to Gander. I was curious to know if my mother would even go through with those rituals on this most sacred of days with such sins on her soul. She did. I knew what I saw to be real because of one simple fact. Back in the summer before I went to the hall, while exchanging confidences with my best friend, Bertha, she told me that she had overheard her parents talking the night before. She was very upset by the conversation and couldn't keep it a secret from me. It seems that they had been talking about my mother and an incident that had occurred at a local jewellery store. Apparently, my mother had been caught and then arrested for stealing a very valuable watch. My stepfather had to pay a substantial fine to keep her from serving jail time. This had not been her first offence. The jeweller had wanted her prosecuted to the fullest extent of the law because he was pretty sure that this had not been her first theft from his store. I got very angry with my friend, accused her of lying and we didn't speak for days. We did eventually make up, as most eleven-year-old girls do, but she didn't take her story back. I put it out of my mind, knowing in my heart that it couldn't possibly be true.

But now here I was, two years later, with no choice but to believe what she'd said and what I'd seen with my own eyes. Other things started falling into place. All the beautiful matching outfits, skirts, blouses, dresses and shoes that I had been wearing every day at the hall were further proof. Yes, I had a pension from my father, but now realized that my stepfather would never have willingly splashed out that kind of money on me. He made good money at this job, but he would never have spent it on me. She often gave me two outfits which were exactly alike but in different colours. So many things made sense now. In my bed in the basement that Easter, I couldn't have gotten more than a few hours' sleep for the whole two weeks that I was at home. I cried and tossed and turned, but mostly I prayed to God to save her soul and to have her saved from eternal damnation.

I thought about all the endless bags that she brought into the house after every shopping trip and realized that probably very little had ever been paid for. There was no financial hardship in our lives. My sister was off on her own working. I just couldn't make any sense of it. I knew very little about the concept of kleptomania and now realize that with her it wasn't a disease. It was just greed, plain and simple. My mother put great stock in appearances. She always had to have the best of everything, more than anyone else, better than anyone else. I researched the disease when I got back to the hall. I had noticed her sense of elation after she had committed her crime, but I was not at all convinced that she was suffering from a psychological ailment. I'm still not.

CHRONICLES OF THE HALL

I was consumed with shame. I realized by then that a lot of people in our small town knew about my mother's crimes. At the end of Easter vacation, I was so happy to get away from her. For a time, I tried to understand what had made her do the things that she did; not just the theft but the way she treated me and the way she treated others, talked about them and put them down. One day, many years later, a psychologist laid a magic word before me that explained it all. Narcissist. In later years, I came to know that other parents were guilty of far worse crimes but back then I believed her to be the worst criminal imaginable. She continued those activities for many years afterwards. When I confronted her about it some years later, she had no defence. What was there to say, after all? And so, when I returned to the hall after that Easter vacation I'd lost faith, not only in the nuns and my mother and the church, but in life itself. I just stopped caring.

Twenty-nine

ON THE LAST DAY SCHOOL, ON MY final walk to the candy store, I committed one final act of defiance. I was not the only one who had been disillusioned by the events of the school year. Most students were just worn out from the brutal shifts and study habits that we had to follow just to get through. I left the last class with my books and, along with hundreds of other students, ripped them to pieces and littered Bonaventure Avenue with the shredded remains. It was the most destructive act that I'd ever committed, and it felt great. The street was a sight of complete carnage and there wasn't a thing that anyone could do about it, particularly the nuns.

I'd spent three years testing the waters of independence and I was still afloat. I often sought freedom from the rules and regulations imposed upon me, but they never did crush my spirit, at least not wholly. I had come close a few times to losing that spirit, but in the end I survived.

I was taught proper elocution, given the opportunity to use my finely trained mind (yes, some of it did sink in) and learned how to live with others in a way that may have been unnatural but stood me in good stead for the years that were to come. I'd learned how to sacrifice a lot in every aspect of my life. The nuns were strong, forceful disciplinarians who we were ill-equipped to face life in the modern and fast-changing world of the late 1960s. We had to tackle that all on our own. Life in an all-girls school leaves one unprepared and uncomfortable in a world full of men. Yes, Vatican II had changed life for those women too, but they forgot to take us along with them into a new world. We left the hall in the face of a sexual revolution. I left as pure in body as I was when I had first walked through the doors.

Those nuns took vows to nurture and educate children to the best of their abilities. In the end, most of them failed miserably. They may have entered religious life with the best of intentions, but they tried to raise us in their own image and somehow forgot that most of us needed tools and skills to make it in the real world.

Some were extraordinary women, who went above and beyond their calling to make our lives better, but those nuns were too few and far between. Most of those special women left the convent long ago, no doubt as disillusioned as we were.

I was happy to hear that they had gone on to marry, teach and have children of their own. They deserved every happiness after the stifling life that they'd had to endure in the convent.

Like most orders, the Sisters of Mercy's numbers have dwindled considerably in recent years. They have had to adapt to life in a more contemporary world. As they did in the past, they still do missionary work in remote parts of the world, but education, the primary foundation of their order, is no longer their main goal. In this changing world there is no place for the restrictive ways that they once imposed on young minds. They are still active in music education, in ecology, in fighting injustice and in women's rights.

Belvedere Orphanage closed in 1969, but the building itself remained in use as government offices until it was abandoned. It was a beautiful old building, built in the Second Empire style, and the third-oldest building in the city. It had once been surrounded by the most beautiful formal gardens in the city. Unfortunately, the orphans were not allowed to enjoy its beauty, but were instead forced to spend their recreation time at the back of the building, with dirt being their only toy.

McAuley Hall no longer exists. It seems as if it's very existence has been erased from the face of the earth. Not even Google Search shows any information on its existence. It remained open for a few years after I left, housing Catholic girls who commuted to Memorial University by bus. To my knowledge, it remained empty for a few years and was then torn down. At present, nothing lies in its place. It's just another scar on the landscape of the ever-dwindling properties of the Roman Catholic Church, no doubt awaiting a wealthy developer's condominiums. There is no trace of the driveway or the overpass, nor can any reference be found about the hall in the history of the Sisters of Mercy. There is now a facility on the grounds of Littledale (the old Mercy Novitiate) called McAuley Convent that houses aging and infirmed nuns. This building lies on the outskirts of the city.

Holy Heart of Mary Regional High School remains, and now educates students of both sexes behind it's now sixty-year-old walls. Changing from its once-overcrowded halls teeming with good Catholic girls to a co-ed institution is a leap that my mind finds difficult to comprehend. The little covered porch, where the girls used to have necking sessions with their boyfriends, has now been removed. Hundreds of cars belonging to students now line the parking lot and surrounding streets. When I was a student there wasn't a single girl who owned or drove a family car to school.

The scores of wonderful girls who went to McAuley Hall, along with me, have faded away into their own lives, just as I have. I've run into a handful over the years in the most unlikely of places, but after exchanging addresses none of us have ever kept in touch. I believe that most of them left the province, just as I did. I know that a lot were anxious to escape the hall and all its memories. This is my story. Each girl who attended has their own and probably bears no resemblance to mine. But we all have one thing in common. We all lived in and survived the hall.

Dedicated to Aislynn
Anything is possible

Epilogue

BEFORE I BEGAN WRITING THIS MEMOIR, I was under the misguided assumption that it would be a fun romp through the past. Instead, it proved to be a painful and emotional venture. Reliving unhappy memories, some of which were buried until I began to write, was not as easy as I had first thought. The floodgates opened. It did, however, become a therapeutic exercise that helped me to reconcile the past with the present.

My life could have gone in many different directions after a childhood filled with sexual and emotional abuse. The neglect, alone, could well have driven me to a life of self-destruction with drugs or alcohol.

For a while, at least, I went looking for love in all the wrong places. That first summer out of high school I again made some very poor choices. Wayne, who had broken up with me to spend a summer on the road with his buddies, was a thing of the past. I have nothing but fond memories of him despite the breakup. He always treated me with love and respect and I believe he genuinely cared about me. I very quickly met another guy and fell madly in love. Looking back now, I can see that I was in love with the idea of love, which was much more appealing than the reality. He seemed to adore me and that was what mattered most. It became a long-distance relationship. We spent most of our time getting to know each other through daily letters and phone calls. We broke up during Christmas vacation of that same year after discovering that we really didn't like each other very much at all. Being in each other's physical presence was certainly not as romantic as our sappy love letters. It was nowhere near as idyllic as we had hoped for, and by Christmas Day we both knew that the love story was over. I was spending the vacation with his family and a return plane ticket that kept me trapped there until well after the New Year. He left me on our last night together on the basement floor of his sister's home, battered, bruised and broken after violently raping me.

I told no one, especially not my mother, until many years later. After all, how could I expect her to believe me? It would have been, in her eyes, just another attempt to garner attention. I kept that secret, even from my husband, until many years into our marriage.

I then went on to another relationship that lasted for five years with a man who was twelve years older than me. I met him just a few months after I had turned seventeen. He was thirty. It doesn't seem like such a huge gap now, but he was divorced and definitely a man of the world. Our relationship was characterized by control and mental and physical abuse. He was unfaithful hundreds of times, a pathological liar and a sociopath with psychotic tendencies. I lived a nightmare for all of our years together. In the beginning, he no doubt picked me because I was easy prey. I was just a girl, disenfranchised from her family, young and vulnerable and obviously looking for love. I thought that I had finally found the man of my dreams.

I wasn't his first victim nor was I to be his last. It was only through the guidance of a true friend that I was finally able to escape his clutches somewhat intact. He stalked me for many months afterwards.

Karma is a wonderful thing. The most recent news that I've had of him was that he's just another of those people who eke out an existence begging on the streets of Toronto where we had once lived together.

The man of my dreams quickly became a nightmare. I managed to hold down a job, all the while moving from place to place, one friend's house to another, one relative to another as they all quickly grew sick of his antics. In between times, we lived in our car. I would get violent headaches from lack of food. He never held down a job for more than a few months at a time. I had no home to return to. My boarding house had been my last home. He made me feel as if this was the only life that I deserved. In the end he accepted a job back in Gander, Newfoundland. I quit my job and followed him back home. I spent a month living in the airport before being taken in by a friend. He had gone back to live with his mother. We still stayed together for another year. All of this seems like a bad dream to me now, an impossible life that must have happened to someone else. But it was very real, and I made it through and came out on the other side.

You probably won't be surprised to learn that I've dealt with bouts of depression and anxiety for most of my adult life. I've been diagnosed with PTSD which probably began with the death of my father. I still mourn his loss every day. I wasn't given the opportunity to grieve after his death. I do remember only spending approximately twenty-two days present in the classroom during that year. I came down with every illness under the sun. I was only six, but I remember every day of that horrible year. I was confined to bed for most of it. I contracted hepatitis with added complications and it took a full year for me to regain my strength.

Now I have a wonderful doctor and a great psychologist. Pile onto the death of my dad, the episodes of sexual abuse and the rape, and there you have it: the perfect recipe for post-traumatic stress disorder.

But then I met my husband, who without a doubt saved my life both literally and figuratively. He was aware of some of my past history, but instead of it scaring him off he seemed to love me more because of it. We've now been married for forty-two years, a long time by anybody's standards. These days, few make it that far down the matrimonial path. He's had to put up with a lot, often without understanding the root of most of my problems. He's definitely one of the good guys.

In my early forties I was diagnosed with fibromyalgia. Fibromyalgia is often associated with childhood trauma. I realize now that even at the age of eight or nine I had some of the symptoms of the disease. Chronic pain is a difficult condition to live with and has caused me to give up some of the things that I truly love to do. Writing has made up for it all. It's a powerful outlet for my creativity and allows me to express that deep dark part of myself.

I've spent most of my adult life working, in one way or another, in endeavours that exhibit my creative side. Although I never did get that degree in interior design, I attended college until I was forced to quit because of poor health. I dabbled in it over the years until my body wouldn't cooperate any longer.

I lost two babies to miscarriage but finally ended up with a wonderful son and a granddaughter who is the light of our lives. She's an old soul, who brings us undefinable joy every minute that we spend together.

A friend of a friend has wisely pointed out that there is a prominent misconception that we owe it to our parents to care for them in their declining years, when many of us may not feel that we necessarily received that same love and support growing up.

Much of my story would come as a shock to my mother and she would no doubt be horribly offended by my recollections. We have discussed some of the events of the past during some quiet times together. She actually apologized and asked my forgiveness for the many ways in which she had failed me. She also told me that she should never have remarried and blamed most of her treatment towards me by passing the buck, so to speak, onto my stepfather. I was under no illusions, though. I'd heard most of the same excuses before. In the end, she seemed to have little regard for either of her husbands, blaming them for her various mistakes and transgressions. A few years later, during an argument, she denied ever apologizing in the first place.

The events of the past made me into who I am today. I was well established in the best part of my life and decided to make hers a little easier. I felt no need to punish. About ten years ago we brought her to live with us. She left the province of her birth, where she'd spent eighty-five years of her life. It was not an easy transition for either of us. But a mother is a mother after all, and in all truthfulness, nobody else wanted to be responsible for her care. She is now living out her days in a home for the aged confined to a wheelchair, incontinent and suffering from the advanced stages of Alzheimer's disease. The years prior that she did spend with us were difficult ones, often hell on earth.

But all in all, I've survived to tell my tale. I hope you enjoyed it.

Acknowledgments

THIS BOOK WOULD NOT HAVE BECOME A reality without the unfailing and unwavering support of the members of WWI (Whitney Writer's Ink). Your constant encouragement has been my biggest inspiration. You kept me moving forward even when I lost faith in myself.

Many thanks to my beta readers: Sandra Dunn, Tricia MacKinnon and Rob Parsons (also, website designer extraordinaire). From the word "go" you loved what you read, gave me priceless feedback and filled me with confidence.

I have steadfast friends, who although not having read the book as of yet, have been nothing but loyal and full of confidence that I could complete this project through to the end, never doubting that I had the talent and fortitude to see it completed. Each and every one of you know who you are. Linda, special thanks goes to you for your chauffeuring and research assistance, not to mention your many years of devoted friendship.

Despite everything, I must thank the Sisters of Mercy and the Sisters of Presentation who gave me the gift of a fine education. I'm sure that their goal was not to make me as stubborn as a mule, but they did and it's seen me through some of the most difficult times of my life. The same can be said of my mother. I am what I am because of you. I'm sure it's not what you intended. I don't really know what your intentions were but whatever they may have been, good or bad, I'm a better person because of them.

The girls of McAuley Hall, unknowingly to them, have been with me every step of the way in this process. I hold them near and dear, and hope that upon reading this memoir I make them laugh or cry and feel and remember.

Last, always and best, to my one true love, Joe, goes my deepest gratitude. I know my dark side scares you, but you put up with it anyway, and have always believed that this project (and anything else that I do) will be a wonderful success. What wife could want for anything more? Daniel, my son, has been no less supportive and confident. In his enthusiasm he's already cast the movie! I love it and him unconditionally.

To my present and future readers, where would I be without you all? Stay tuned for future works and follow me on social media at christinemackinnon.ca for further links and news of upcoming projects. It's also a way to get to know me a little better.

A native of Newfoundland, Christine currently lives in Nova Scotia. Writing is her passion and takes up most of her time. Travelling is one of her other great loves. Her works have been published in several anthologies and magazines and she is currently working on her second novel, entitled *Sarah's Settle*.